RAISING CONTRIBUTORS

IN A CULTURE OF
CONSUMERISM AND SKEPTICISM

DR. BRANDON TATUM

ISBN 979-8-88751-647-9 (paperback)
ISBN 979-8-88751-648-6 (digital)

Copyright © 2023 by Dr. Brandon Tatum

All rights reserved. No part of this publication may be reproduced, distributed, or transmitted in any form or by any means, including photocopying, recording, or other electronic or mechanical methods without the prior written permission of the publisher. For permission requests, solicit the publisher via the address below.

Christian Faith Publishing
832 Park Avenue
Meadville, PA 16335
www.christianfaithpublishing.com

Printed in the United States of America

CONTENTS

Introduction v
Chapter 1: Generations Alpha and Z 1

Section 1: Raising Contributors in a Culture of Consumption 9

Chapter 2: Who Are These Kids? 11
Chapter 3: Living in a Broken Culture of Parenting 30
Chapter 4: A More Hopeful Parenting Culture 54
Chapter 5: Called to Contribute 68

Section 2: Raising Contributors in a Culture of Skepticism 83

Part 2 Introduction 85
Chapter 6: Meaning and Truth 87
Chapter 7: What Is Real? 107
Chapter 8: Demons, Ghosts, and Magic 119
Chapter 9: So What Now? 130
Chapter 10: The Playbook How to Raise a Contributor 140

Bibliography 155

INTRODUCTION

Thanks for picking up the book! Hopefully, you are coming to this book with a bit of curiosity. Maybe you are curious about this upcoming generation of emerging adults, maybe you are curious about how to navigate the parenting landscape of the twenty-first century, maybe you are curious to understand the culture in which our kids are living, or maybe you just want to know how to cultivate contribution in your child. I don't know what brings you to this book, but I hope you will enjoy taking a tour through history and a deep dive into this inspiring generation of kids.

Faith has always been an important element in my life. How we are to raise our kids within the context of the Christian faith has become of particular interest to me since having children. I have three children who are all in elementary school and part of Generation Alpha. This book is written through the lens of the Christian faith and how we are to raise up faith contributors for the kingdom. The first chapter spends a significant amount of time describing Generations Alpha and Z to help you better understand them. However, allow me to provide a bit of context in the introduction.

Recently, I came across a fascinating article from 1922. It was written by a teenager of that day named Ellen Page and was published in *Outlook* magazine. Ellen Page wrote, "I want to beg all you parents, and grandparents, and friends, and teachers, and preachers—you who constitute the "older generation"—to overlook our shortcomings, at least for the present, and to appreciate our virtues." She went on, "Instead of helping us work out our problems with constructive, sympathetic thinking and acting, you have muddled them for us more hopelessly with destructive public condemnation."

I love how she calls out the older generations and pleads that they appreciate the virtues of her generation. Whether it's 1922 or today, the fact is, kids will be kids, and the older generation will always believe in the degradation of the newer generation. You must admit, the millennial generation got a pretty bad rap! How many millennial Facebook posts or videos have you forwarded or shared recently attacking that generation? It's funny to me that this has seemed to always be the case, and even in 1922, the older generation believed their younger generation was a mess.

She continued:

> We have a tremendous problem on our hands. You must help us. Give us confidence—not distrust. Give us practical aid and advice—not criticism. Praise us when praise is merited. Be patient and understanding when we make mistakes. Spiritual forces begin to be felt. The emotions are frequently in a state of upheaval, struggling with one another for supremacy. And youth does not understand. There is no one to turn to—no one but the rest of youth, which is as perplexed and troubled with its problems as ourselves. Everywhere we read and hear the criticism and distrust of older people toward us. It forms an insurmountable barrier between us. How can we turn to them? In every person there is a desire, an innate longing, toward some special goal or achievement. Each of us has his place to fill. Each of us has his talent—be it ever so humble. That is why it is up to you who have the supervision of us of less ripe experience to guide us sympathetically, and to help us find, encourage, and develop our special abilities and talents. Study us. Make us realize that you respect us as fellow

RAISING CONTRIBUTORS
IN A CULTURE OF CONSUMERISM AND SKEPTICISM

human beings, that you have confidence in us, and, above all, that you expect us to live up to the highest ideals, and to the best that is in us. Oh, parents, parents everywhere, point out to us the ideals of truly glorious and upright living! Believe in us, that we may learn to believe in ourselves, in humanity, in God! Be the living examples of your teachings, that you may inspire us with hope and courage, understanding and truth, love and faith. Remember that we are the parents of the future. Help us to be worthy of the sacred trust that will be ours. Make your lives such an inspiration to us that we in turn will strive to become an inspiration to our children and to the ages! Is it too much to ask?

This young teenage girl from 1922 urges, pleads, and inspires each of us today to be examples for our younger generation. It is a powerful reminder that we should all take to heart. Ellen is no different than any kid today. She had big dreams and was committed to being a virtuous and good person. She strived to be a good mother one day and a citizen that made a real impact on the world. She truly desired to contribute in some meaningful way. She, like our kids today, was confused, scared, and looked around her culture asking many questions. In so many ways, Ellen's experience is identical to that of Generation Z but in other ways, worlds apart.

This book will be full of strategies and tactics for forming our kids, but I want to put Ellen's words at the beginning because no strategy works if we are not living out the life God has called us to as adults and mentors. As adults, we can gripe about the next generation, we can complain and roll our eyes at the way they are doing life, but we must remember that we are called by our Creator to develop our children into the likeness of Christ. We must cultivate their contribution, ability, and skills. To me, everything in faith formation for the emerging generations comes back to the concept of contribution. Why? Because raising contributors matters. Help them identify, foster, and build upon their gifts. Provide them opportunities to contribute to society.

Before we begin, let me spend some time defining what being a contributor means. A contributor is someone who lives into their God-given mission for their life. They are people who are image bearers, difference makers, and who participate in making the world around them better. They are not self-seeking or self-focused; rather, they are committed to others beyond themselves. They are kingdom-focused individuals that contribute to society. Mr. Rogers would define a contribution lifestyle like this, "The purpose of life is to listen—to yourself, to your neighbor, to your world and to God and, when the time comes, to respond in as helpful a way as you can find…from within and without."

Parents, youth leaders, teachers, ministers, grandparents, and anyone who loves kids, take this book as a call to be bold and believe in this generation because they can be amazing contributors!

CHAPTER 1

Generations Alpha and Z

> "Please think of the children first. If you ever have anything to do with their entertainment, their food, their toys, their custody, their child care, their health care, their education—listen to the children, learn about them, learn from them. Think of the children first."
>
> —Mr. Rogers

I have been inspired to write this book for a couple of reasons. First of all, my three children inspire me every day to be a better dad and mentor to them. As I am raising them in what seems to be a very different world than the one I grew up in, I am empowered to learn how a parent should navigate this consumer-centric culture. They are bombarded with temptations, devices, and a culture concerned with only one thing—fostering consumption. Before I had children, I had lofty hopes to create a family culture where we would donate our birthday presents to those more needy or have a Christmas truly focused on the birth of Jesus and not toys. As a dad now, I have utterly failed at those lofty goals. The truth of the matter is that I am more of a greedy consumer than even my children! There are, however, ways we can practically navigate this world we are in, and I hope to share some of that because this consumption culture is obviously remapping the brains of our children.

Secondly, I am inspired by the questions that I am asked on a normal basis from parents and grandparents. For two decades I have been working with children. I started out as a high school basketball coach and teacher, then began to work with college kids as a basketball coach, then became a K-12 superintendent. This last experience allowed me to be completely embedded into the lives of kids. Now, I serve as college administrator and love getting to see how college kids are attempting to navigate the world. The questions I am asked are the typical questions:

- How do I protect my kids from this evil and liberal culture?
- How do I make sure my children are safe?
- What do I do when my child is addicted to their phone?
- When should my kids get their first iPad or iPhone?
- How do I monitor my kids' technology?
- Help! My child is questioning God!
- Help! My child does not believe in the Bible anymore! How did this happen?

The questions range from practical questions about technology to the deeper questions about faith and life. There is a big move for many parents trying to protect their children from a lot of this, and I want to spend a significant amount of time unpacking that strategy.

As mentioned, while I have spent a lot of time around kids, I am still struggling to figure all of this out as a father. As I write this, my Generation Alpha children are in elementary school. In many ways, the old adage rings true—*it's easier said than done*. It is much easier to write a book about how we are to navigate the world as a parent than actually implementing the perfect parenting strategy. Fortunately, there is no perfect parenting strategy! We are nothing as parents unless we lean on God during this scary parenting journey.

So I am an imperfect father, and I am also a recovering millennial. I am not sure how I have survived my millennialism, but as for now, I seem to be navigating life fairly well. I suppose the best advice I have ever received on surviving millennialism came from Dr. Leo Marvin as he told Bob in *What About Bob*, "Just take baby steps." I

RAISING CONTRIBUTORS
IN A CULTURE OF CONSUMERISM AND SKEPTICISM

tell myself this each morning I wake up. Often, I am embarrassed that I am a millennial. We just have been given a pretty bad rap by older generations. So let me now admit I am Brandon Tatum, and I'm a millennial. Yes, I was born in 1984, so arguably, I am an older millennial, but regardless, I'm one of them. Why is this important to note? I believe I am one of the few millennial researchers trying to understand and engage the younger generations. In a way, I share many of the same theological pains as Generation Z and probably similar pains to this new generation emerging behind them. I hope to possibly remedy this pain for my children and students through becoming an understanding and intentional adult in regard to their faith formation.

Currently, we are in the process of raising two generations. Our middle schoolers, high schoolers, and college students are a part of Generation Z. Our elementary-age students and below are a part of what we are calling Generation Alpha. So we will spend some time trying to take a holistic look at this group of kids. Due to their age, we will spend a significant amount of time on Generation Z, but I will discuss what I know about Generation Alpha and the world they have been born into:

- I think Generation Z lives within a context of low expectations.
- I think Generation Z lives in a world of consumption.
- I think Generation Z lives in a world where what other people think about them matters.
- I think Generation Z lives in a state of anxiety due to social networks.
- I think Generation Z lives in a world of financial awareness.
- I think Generation Z lives in a world that is confused about the spiritual realm.
- I think Generation Z lives in a tension between a literate and a visual culture.
- I think Generation Z lives in a socially, emotionally, and physically confusing moment.

- And I think Generation Alpha has been born into all of this mess.

Generations Alpha and Z are a diverse group of children that we are called to disciple. As parents, grandparents, educators, and church leaders, we must develop an understanding of new expectations for our kids and provide a framework of reconstructing new practices. We will discuss the necessary expectations our kids need to be functional adults in society, but we will also look at expectations to help develop our children spiritually.

I also like to mention when I talk about generational data and statistics that I am speaking in generalities. This somewhat stereotypical conversation can be offensive to some that may find themselves as an outlier of the aggregate data, so for those individuals, I apologize. I can also empathize with these outliers because I find myself as an outlier of the millennial generation. It is also important that I note the differences between generational findings and human development. Erik Erikson has developed eight life stages that we tend to fall in as we age:

- Stage 1: Infant to eighteen months (trust vs. mistrust)
- Stage 2: Eighteen months to three years (autonomy vs. shame and doubt)
- Stage 3: Three years to five years (initiative vs. guilt)
- Stage 4: Five years to thirteen years (industry vs. inferiority)
- Stage 5: Thirteen years to twenty-one years (identity vs. role confusion)
- Stage 6: Twenty-one years to thirty-nine years (intimacy vs. isolation)
- Stage 7: Thirty-nine years to sixty-five years (generativity vs. stagnation)
- Stage 8: Sixty-five years and older (ego integrity vs. despair)

I will refer to these life stages throughout the book because it's important to remember that while some things are generational, others are just age specific. So we may say things like, "Well, that younger generation is so indecisive." However, you were probably indecisive at that age too! In other words, there are just some things that thirteen-year-olds deal with no matter the generation, and we should be self-reflective and empathetic in these areas.

In this light, there are developmental concerns that sociologists are seeing too. We know from anecdotal and personal life experiences that we are seeing childhood become prolonged into the late twenties to early thirties. We see teenagers getting their driver's license later, college graduates moving home upon graduation, marriages happening later in life, and the list could continue. What's fascinating is that from my experience as an educator, I am seeing students being exposed to life earlier and earlier but developing emotionally later and later.

For a generation like Generation X, your experience would have looked like this. Generation X was more closely exposed to age-related realities within each of these educational categories.

Elementary School	Middle School	High School

From an exposure point of view, we are seeing this type of pattern for our emerging generations.

Middle School in Elementary	High School in Middle School	College in High School

Developmentally, we are seeing puberty hitting our youth earlier, and for some young ladies, this can start taking place in early elementary. We know many of our students will be exposed to pornography in elementary school, predominately on accident through the unsupervised use of technology. While they are being exposed to the harsh realities of life at an earlier age, it is not manifesting in a more mature group of kids. In fact, it is evident that they are not mentally prepared to handle the emotional realities they are facing and so we see emotional distress and unpreparedness with them. In fact, while they may be experiencing college-like events in high school, they are graduating high school overwhelmed and stressed.

From a faith perspective, Barna Group has done significant research in recent years on Generation Z. Their findings and their statistical analyses are always interesting to me. I had the chance to visit with David Kinnaman, president of Barna, and he was telling me that at face value, Generation Z seems very similar to the millennial generation. However, as you peel back the layers, we find a much-different group. According to Barna research from their book *Gen Z*, we find these findings on Gen Z spirituality:

- Teens thirteen to eighteen years old are twice as likely as adults to say they are atheist (13 percent vs. 6 percent).
- Half say happiness is their ultimate goal in life (51 percent).
- Only 9 percent of Generation Z are engaged Christians. Engaged Christians are the only faith segment likely to say faith is central to their identity, and few teens overall see spiritual maturity as a worthy ambition.
- One-quarter of Gen Z strongly agrees that what is morally right and wrong changes over time based on society, and they are nearly on par with millennials in believing each individual is his or her own moral arbiter.
- Three out of five among the eldest generation strongly agree that lying is immoral, while only one-third of Gen Z believes lying is wrong.
- Only about one in four among all Gen Z believes science and the Bible are complementary (28 percent).
- Four out of five churchgoing teens say church is relevant to them (82 percent).
- More than one-third of Gen Z believes it is not possible to know for sure if God is real (37 percent), compared to 32 percent of all adults.
- Nearly half of teens, on par with millennials, say, "I need factual evidence to support my beliefs" (46 percent)—which helps to explain their uneasiness with the relationship between science and the Bible.

RAISING CONTRIBUTORS IN A CULTURE OF CONSUMERISM AND SKEPTICISM

Overall, we are continuing to see a shift in spirituality with the younger generations. I remember a decade ago reading and then presenting the data out of Kendra Dean's book *Almost Christian* as she brought to light the work of Dr. Christian Smith. Dr. Smith laid the groundwork that we are losing our children. The fascinating thing to me is that not much has changed in our churches, homes, or schools based on the plethora of research suggesting we are losing the spiritual battle. Great researchers like Kendra Dean, Dr. Christian Smith, Dr. Tim Elmore, David Kinnaman, and Gabe Lyons have all been ringing the alarm bells for the past decade, and it's time we listen!

PART 1

Raising Contributors in a Culture of Consumption

CHAPTER 2

Who Are These Kids?

What we see and hear on the screen is part of who we become.

—Mr. Rogers

From Grandpa to Jason

On the 8th day, God looked down on his planned paradise and said, "I need a caretaker." So God made a farmer.

God said, "I need somebody willing to get up before dawn, milk cows, work all day in the fields, milk cows again, eat supper and then go to town and stay past midnight at a meeting of the school board." So God made a farmer.

"I need somebody with arms strong enough to rustle a calf and yet gentle enough to deliver his own grandchild. Somebody to call hogs, tame cantankerous machinery, come home hungry, have to wait for lunch until his wife's done feeding visiting ladies and tell the ladies to be sure and come back real soon—and mean it." So God made a farmer.

God said, "I need somebody willing to sit up all night with a newborn colt. And watch it die. Then dry his eyes and say, 'Maybe next year.' I need somebody who can shape an ax handle from a persimmon sprout, shoe a horse with a hunk of car tire, who can make harnesses out of haywire, feed sacks and shoe scraps. And who, planting time and harvest season, will finish his forty-hour week by Tuesday noon, then, pain'n from 'tractor back,' put in another seventy-two hours." So God made a farmer.

God had to have somebody willing to ride the ruts at double speed to get the hay in ahead of the rain clouds and yet stop in mid-field and race to help when he sees the first smoke from a neighbor's place. So God made a farmer.

God said, "I need somebody strong enough to clear trees and heave bails, yet gentle enough to tame lambs and wean pigs and tend the pink-combed pullets, who will stop his mower for an hour to splint the broken leg of a meadowlark. It had to be somebody who'd plow deep and straight and not cut corners. Somebody to seed, weed, feed, breed and rake and disc and plow and plant and tie the fleece and strain the milk and replenish the self-feeder and finish a hard week's work with a five-mile drive to church.

"Somebody who'd bale a family together with the soft strong bonds of sharing, who would laugh and then sigh, and then reply, with smiling

RAISING CONTRIBUTORS
IN A CULTURE OF CONSUMERISM AND SKEPTICISM

eyes, when his son says he wants to spend his life 'doing what dad does.'" So God made a farmer.

In 2019, Americans were reminded of this 1978 speech given by Paul Harvey to the Future Farmers of America. The speech was the soundtrack to a Dodge Ram commercial during Super Bowl Sunday. There is a special place in our hearts for farmers and for the men and women that work hard so that we can put food on our table.

Farm to table is a new phenomenon hitting the eating scene across our country. Most Americans like this concept, and we gravitate toward the restaurants that have adopted this concept. We find the food from farms to be fresh, free of pesticides, and we feel a sense of pride in helping the farmers of our country. There is something pure about the farm because we know the farm illustrates a healthier way of life.

I grew up in a small town outside of Austin, Texas called Pflugerville. It was a small farming community, so many of the kids I knew growing up lived on a farm. As an elementary student, I remember being jealous of how they grew up, but my only knowledge of their lifestyle was after school running in the fields, riding four-wheelers through the woods, and chasing cows across the pasture. It seemed like a kid's paradise for play. Living on the farm seemed idyllic. In my third-grade ignorance, I didn't realize that my friends were up before the sun feeding their animals, cracking ice, shoveling poop, and all the other hard things that come with living on a farm.

Our kids have entered into a much-different world than my farming friends. As parents and grandparents, we know children growing up today are significantly different than a couple of generations ago. We look into the future and worry about our children's work ethic, emotional stability, and their ownership of a deep faith. This book will explore these concerns by asking us to go back in time. Back to a time when children were expected to work, contribute to their family, and make a difference in their world. Since many of us are not raising children on a farm, we must begin to ask ourselves some new questions. What is our new farm? How can I instill the principles of the farm while my kids live in a world of consumption?

As Paul Harvey reminded us, God made the farmer, and God made my great-grandfather. He was born in 1904. Unfortunately, I never got to meet Earl, but his wife, my great-grandmother (Granny Great) was a firecracker of a woman. She had a pink recliner and always wore these pajama-like dresses. I don't think I ever saw her leave her single-wide trailer, and I rarely saw her leave her recliner. For years as a child, I thought Granny Great always had to throw up every few minutes in her trash can by her recliner. I assumed that when you got as old as her, this was a normal part of life. I didn't think much about it except her throw up had a distinct smell, somewhat sweet, and she was great at aiming her throw up right into the middle of the trash can. It wasn't until I was a preteen before I learned that she chewed tobacco. I was relieved to know that I wasn't going to begin throwing up constantly as I aged, and then I kind of thought my Granny Great was cool. Like wow, my great-grandmother is a rule breaker.

Anyways, Earl was one of eight children in his family. He obviously lived through the Great Depression, and like so many, his family was met with significant financial hardship. So in seventh grade, Earl had to drop out of school to begin working on the farm with his father. This work was meant to provide for his family, and he became an active contributor to society. He was married at seventeen years old, had six children of his own, and he ended up with his own farm. He was active in helping his community and church. Earl did not have a spectacular life. He did not become governor of a state or founder of a multimillion-dollar company, but his story mimics that of his generation. A generation that was expected to work and contribute.

It was around 1900 when labor and school reform laws were passed in an attempt to protect kids from the difficult working environment of the factories. This was probably a needed move to protect our youth, and I am not suggesting we go back to child labor. However, these teen workers who were expected to play a role in helping their communities and families began to experience a lack of expectation in their lives, and these expectations are dropping further and further down the generational ladder. It was also in the book,

RAISING CONTRIBUTORS
IN A CULTURE OF CONSUMERISM AND SKEPTICISM

Do Hard Things, that I learned of the first usage of the term *teenager*. Teenager was first used in a 1941 *Reader's Digest* article.

As you think about it, before this time, there was really no need to have a title for this subpopulation. Prior to the reform and labor laws, you really were either a child or an adult, and this would have been true for most of the world and human history. The concept of having *teenagers* is still less than one hundred years old. This is why the apostle Paul wrote, "When I was a child, I talked like a child, I thought like a child, I reasoned like a child. When I became a man, I put the ways of childhood behind me" (1 Corinthians 13:11). You notice how it's only child and adult. There is no phase of life where we live in the *in-between*. As an American culture, this is new to us.

Dr. Markella Rutherford examined societal expectations of children through historically reviewing the *Parents* magazine:

> She found that though the 1930's, 40's, and 50's chores were a common subject in articles written by experts and laypeople alike; children were doing much work to maintain a household, including fire-tending, meal preparation, carpentry, maintaining household accounts, and looking after sick family members. Chores all but dropped out of *Parents* magazine discourse in the 1960's, 70's, and 80's. When, in the 1990's, articles in *Parents* about chores returned as a topic of expert and lay opinion, the chores references were 'trivial tasks' compared to the chores done by children in the earlier decades.

Sometimes, we look back in time with an idyllic sense. We are very egotistical in a sense because we think that no generation has had it as bad as we have it, or we think that the challenges of today don't compare with the challenges of yesterday. Well, if that's how you think, you should reconsider. Take a step back in time and look at life during Grandpa Earl's years.

Cultural events that happened within my great-grandfather's lifetime:

- 1901—President McKinley assassinated
- 1901—Walt Disney born
- 1902—First Rose Bowl game played
- 1903—*Great Train Robbery* movie opens
- 1903—Harley-Davidson Motor Company created
- 1903—Ford Motor Company formed
- 1903—First World Series
- 1906—San Francisco earthquake
- 1907—Coal mine explodes in Monongah, West Virginia, killing at least 361; worst industrial accident in American history
- 1908—Ford Model T appears on market
- 1909—Pinchot-Ballinger controversy
- 1912—RMS *Titanic* sinks
- 1912—Theodore Roosevelt shot, but not killed, while campaigning for the Bull Moose Party
- 1912—Vice President Sherman dies
- 1917—US enters World War I
- 1919—18th Amendment, establishing Prohibition
- 1919—Black Sox Scandal during that year's World Series, with the fallout lasting for decades
- 1920—First radio broadcasts by KDKA in Pittsburgh and WWJ in Detroit
- 1920—Economy collapses; depression of 1920–21 begins
- 1920—National Football League is formed
- 1923—Teapot Dome scandal
- 1924—Immigration Act Basic Law
- 1928—Disney's *Steamboat Willie* opens, the first animated picture to feature Mickey Mouse
- 1929—St. Valentine's Day Massacre
- 1929—The Dow Jones Industrial Average plummets a record sixty-eight points over a two-day period, setting off the Wall Street Crash of 1929 and triggering the Great Depression

RAISING CONTRIBUTORS
IN A CULTURE OF CONSUMERISM AND SKEPTICISM

Anytime researchers discuss generations, it is understood that generational cohorts are a bit blurry. My great-grandfather was a part of the GI generation. Most agree that the millennial generation starts in the early 1980s. There are two different camps of Gen Z researchers giving birth years. One group of researchers put their birth date around 2001 while others are focused on 1995. When I started with my research, I used the 2001 date to classify Gen Z because it seemed to logically coincide with two major cultural events. The most obvious world-changing event happened on September 11, 2001 in New York City. The next major cultural phenomenon was the infusion of the *i* technology—iPod, iTouch. These two life-altering occurrences changed our world forever, and researchers like to start generational cohorts around prominent cultural events.

After more research and life experience, however, I have begun using 1995 as the start date for Generation Z. The differences in what some would call young millennials and older millennials is pretty drastic, and while 2001 provided a major cultural event, 1995 offered a technological and entertainment explosion. On November 22, 1995, Pixar's *Toy Story* hit theaters and was the highest grossing film on its opening weekend, earning over $373 million worldwide.

Generation Alpha is still very young as I write this. We do not know as much about their generational outcomes, but we know a lot about the world they are growing up in. Generation Alpha was born around 2010 and is the first generation to be born entirely in the twenty-first century. That fact is going to be critical in trying to understand them and how they will be approaching their spiritual walk. Most members of Generation Alpha have millennial parents, such as myself. This group of kids have lived in a world where they only know about iPhones, iPads, social networks, and streaming entertainment. Just to remind you, the iPhone and iPad were released in 2007 right before this generation emerged on the scene. By the time they hit elementary school, personal technology had hit new heights in usage, and the entertainment industry exploded around them.

I'm really excited to have these generations invading our lives because they bring a lively spirit, a heart for others, and a healthy understanding of change. They are a tribe which is identified by the experiences they have had, and sadly, not the qualities they have developed because of those experiences. The social media influence of this generation has become an identifiable trait.

Now, let's now compare a teenager today against the framework of my great-grandfather. Let's use a teenager named Jason. Jason will spend on average nine hours a day online according to Common Sense Media. Teen boys will spend fifty-six minutes a day playing video games. American companies alone will spend upward of seventeen billion dollars marketing to these kids. According to an article from CNN, they have the family spending purchasing power of $600 billion in the market.

Jason goes to school every day and is overly pushed by his parents to get all As even though realistically, he is probably a B student. Jason plays a lot of sports. In fact, he has been playing baseball and basketball since he was three years old. He travels regularly for tournaments, and his family is away most weekends playing one of those sports depending on the season. He doesn't have to work and really doesn't have time for work with all the video games, practices, and schoolwork he has to do. Statistically, Jason will feel overwhelmed with life and stressed out to his max. His parents are around and involved in his life but are emotionally disconnected from him. They feel close to him because they are at all of his events, but a deep and meaningful relationship is nonexistent.

The differences between my great-grandfather's childhood and Jason's childhood are stark. We also know that the outcomes of these two generations are significantly different. We know that statistically, Generation Z is dealing with the highest levels of anxiety and depression, they are maturing much later in life and putting off adulthood, and they are leaving their faith at alarmingly high rates. The question is, why? Why is this happening? Some researchers would say we got here through the social and cultural events of the day. So what has this generation experienced?

RAISING CONTRIBUTORS
IN A CULTURE OF CONSUMERISM AND SKEPTICISM

These generations have experienced war

They have experienced a lot in their short lifetimes. In fact, many call Generation Z the *Homeland Generation* due to the nature of terrorism they have experienced, and Generation Alpha will have a lot of connectivity to COVID-19 and how it has influenced them. Regardless of their birth year, we must recognize that they have grown up in a post-9/11 world which is far different than even the world I grew up in. I am old enough to remember the ease of airport security, going to a professional or college game without metal detectors, and playing cowboys with toy guns in elementary school. In many ways, the current cultural context is fear driven and safety focused.

While 9/11 changed our country, we must remember that these students live in a post-Columbine world as well. I would argue for older generations school life was experienced with no fear of being shot at school. However, this is a grim reality for our current students. As an educator, this is my greatest fear and as an adult can cause me great anxiety many days. I can't imagine the cognitive angst this causes in the lives of our children. Shooter drills are a common part of their school life, being buzzed into buildings with access control, being watched on cameras, and in some school settings, walking through metal detectors each morning.

These generations have experienced a financial crisis

They have also experienced a major downturn in the economy, war, heightened racial tensions, major social issues, and a significant amount of pluralistic faith experiences. These events have resulted in a generation that potentially values fiscal responsibility, tolerance of others, education, employment flexibility, and networking abilities. Typically, difficult times experienced within culture bring people together, and this seems to be true for Generation Z. Due to the world they have been brought up in, they should place a strong emphasis on issues of social justice and creating a better world.

This generation will also be known for fiscal responsibility unlike the previous generation. While millennials wanted to go to the college with the biggest and best recreation center, this generation is looking at the price tag. While they still want nice facilities, the amenities do not seem to be the driving force. They are interested in their careers and the financial security they will have. Security seems to be a strong word to sum up this generation because of earlier mentioned reasons and this need to be financially secure.

I remember sitting in IHOP writing this book while a high school kid in the booth in front of me was visiting with what sounded like his youth minister. The boy began talking about how his dad had been laid off for a second time and how the boy's lawn-mowing business had become a source of income for the family. The weight of this was hard for the boy to carry, and the stress was heavy on his mind. The journey of a parent being laid off is the story for so many kids in this generation since they lived through the financial crisis and the instability of the market.

The desire to obtain a college degree for this generation is high, but they are much more practical in their decision-making when choosing a college. How much debt will I get? What are the average salaries graduating from a specific program? What are the acceptance rates of graduate programs? What are the success rates for certifications? These are some of the many practical questions being asked by this group. With that said, trade school is very promising for many in this generation. It is a practical step with an immediate return on investment.

These generations have experienced different family systems

As an overgeneralization, these kids are experiencing a much-different family system than previous generations. So far, both Generations Alpha and Z are the most fragmented and varied generations. Their worlds are defined by the internet, globalization and the multiculturalism associated with this, terrorism, the financial crisis, the breakdown of the family, and essentially a complete loss of security. Security, there is that word again. Grandparents raising grandkids is on the rise, the percentage of divorced families continues to increase, the foster and adoption system is seeing increases within their programs, there is fluidity around gender roles, and the list of family differences could continue. The point is that these emerging generations are likely going to have a difficult time trusting the adults in their lives.

These generations have experienced a technological explosion

Many researchers use the term *digital natives* because they are growing up in the age of social media. Fortunately, both Generations Alpha and Z have a great opportunity to learn from the devastating use of social media that their millennial friends and older siblings experience. While millennials had social media thrown at them in a way that they could only experiment with and fail, in many ways, Generation Z is showing greater responsibility. Have you ever wondered why there has been a rise in popularity for anonymous social media apps? More than likely, it's because their parents have been posting about them on social media for years, and they have been forced into valuing personal privacy more than older generations. I must admit I am a culprit for posting about my children!

Furthermore, marketing research has identified social media apps as the primary marketing method for these kids. I'm a sucker for social media advertising! The algorithm they use to advertise the things I am interested in is mind-blowing. As you would assume, this new generation is positioned to be a significant market for companies. In fact, marketing experts are projecting this generation to bring in billions of dollars to our economy each year while companies will spend billions of dollars marketing to this population.

Many researchers would say since 9/11, our kids have experienced a world like never before. A world of terror, killings, political scandals, and the list could continue. However, I'm not convinced these cultural events have caused the specific generational outcomes we are seeing. Many researchers and sociologists suggest that the cultural events our kids grew up in significantly impacted the outcomes we experience. But there must be something deeper going on. Why? Because we live in a broken world, and it has been broken for a long time. Did Gen Z experience a war? Yes, but so did other generations.

Did Gen Z see a financial crisis? Yes, but so did other generations. Does Gen Z see racism playing out in our world? Yes, but so did other generations. Cultural events have always been around, but the generational outcomes are drastically different.

As you look at the culture surrounding my great-grandfather and the culture surrounding Jason, it is actually quite similar. Remember this previous list of historical events surrounding my great grandfather's life?

Cultural events that happened within my great-grandfather's lifetime:

- 1901—President McKinley assassinated
- 1901—Walt Disney born
- 1902—First Rose Bowl game played
- 1903—*Great Train Robbery* movie opens
- 1903—Harley-Davidson Motor Company created
- 1903—Ford Motor Company formed
- 1903—First World Series
- 1906—San Francisco earthquake
- 1907—Coal mine explodes in Monongah, West Virginia, killing at least 361; worst industrial accident in American history
- 1908—Ford Model T appears on market
- 1909—Pinchot-Ballinger controversy
- 1912—RMS *Titanic* sinks
- 1912—Theodore Roosevelt shot, but not killed, while campaigning for the Bull Moose Party
- 1912—Vice President Sherman dies
- 1917—US enters World War I
- 1919—18th Amendment, establishing Prohibition
- 1919—Black Sox Scandal during that year's World Series, with the fallout lasting for decades
- 1920—First radio broadcasts by KDKA in Pittsburgh and WWJ in Detroit
- 1920—Economy collapses; depression of 1920–21 begins
- 1920—National Football League is formed

RAISING CONTRIBUTORS IN A CULTURE OF CONSUMERISM AND SKEPTICISM

- 1923—Teapot Dome scandal
- 1924—Immigration Act Basic Law
- 1928—Disney's *Steamboat Willie* opens, the first animated picture to feature Mickey Mouse
- 1929—St. Valentine's Day Massacre
- 1929—The Dow Jones Industrial Average plummets a record sixty-eight points over a two-day period, setting off the Wall Street Crash of 1929 and triggering the Great Depression

Even then we saw war, murder, financial crisis, entertainment, politics, and the list of similarities could go on. Cultural events are not the problem we are facing today. The genesis of our problem lies in the expectations set for our kids. There is one fundamental difference between Earl and Jason. Earl was a key contributor to society, and Jason is a key consumer of society. I want you to hear the deep complexities in the simplicity of that statement. There are considerable implications to this statement. Earl was a key contributor to society, and Jason is a key consumer of society.

What is expected of them?

Essentially, expectations for kids today are the most basic. They are easy, low, and don't train our kids to use many physical or emotional muscles. They are chores that show how little respect we really have for kids and highlight how little we value their ability to contribute at a meaningful level. Allow me to jot down a few I grabbed from a quick Google search.

Preteens: Thirteen to sixteen:

— Managing an allowance.
— Making plans with friends and giving you all of the necessary information.
— Have useful daily habits like making his/her bed and picking up his/her room.

- Cleaning his/her room—vacuuming, dusting, etc.—weekly, with some parental help.

Older teens: Sixteen to nineteen:

- Everything on the preteen list.
- Doing a daily household chore, such as cleaning the dinner dishes, straightening the family room, swiping down the bathroom, etc.
- Make sure the gas gauge in the car does not go below a quarter of a tank.

Our expectations for our children today are laughable. Brothers Alex and Brett Harris wrote a book in 2001 called *Do Hard Things* as they urged their millennial generation to step up and do the hard things for their faith. I appreciated the way in which they highlighted the disconnect between generational expectations. Consider these for a moment:

- In 1800, young people of both sexes would be considered adults as soon as puberty made an outwardly appearance.
- Boys could join the army as an officer cadet at fifteen years old.
- The school leaving age was moved to fourteen years old in the nineteenth century.
- In 1900, one out of ten young American people between fourteen to seventeen years old attended high school.

As we go back to the dichotomy between the way my great-grandfather grew up and Jason, we can compare these two personal narratives, and there is a glaring difference. Again, Earl was a key contributor to society while Jason is a key consumer of society.

It's so easy and tempting to be led down the path of consumption. Our kids are surrounded by it. Marketing groups are bombarding them with advertisements on their social media and app platforms, through YouTube and video game addiction. But let's press

RAISING CONTRIBUTORS
IN A CULTURE OF CONSUMERISM AND SKEPTICISM

pause and come to a realization. Technology, for all of its convenience and improvements to our daily lives, has birthed a kind of on-demand consumerism. It's not their fault they are consumers. We're doing a poor job of making kids appreciative for the conveniences of life. Conveniences like microwaves, televisions, vehicles, air-conditioning, heating, and the list could go on. How do we know our children are consumers? Here are a few outcomes of consumption:

- Obesity among children has increased 500 percent since the 1960s.
- Toy sales that were almost nonexistent in the 1930s have skyrocketed to billions in annual sales today.
- Children thirteen or older spend two-thirds of their lives hooked to devices.
- More and more young American men are dropping out of college because of technology amusements.
- Five million Americans spend forty-five hours a week on video games.
- A recent study by Barna Group highlighted that 63 percent of men between eighteen to thirty view pornography at least once a week.
- Pediatricians are having to create time limits for screen time for kids five years old and younger.

One of my first coaching jobs was at a small college, and in my first year, I recruited about forty kids to come play basketball. Most were coming from out of state, and most were from Texas. Texas is hot, and air-conditioning is nice to have. Interestingly enough, this college did not have air-conditioning in the freshman dorms. It was a relatively cool climate, so A/C wasn't a necessity. However, something interesting happened. My players had to realize the convenience of air-conditioning. They had assumed their entire lives that air-conditioning was a necessity in American life. When do we actually teach our children the differences between necessities and blessings?

By the age of three, my son Sawyer had already learned that he needed every toy in the store or that he needed ice cream in the evening or he needed to watch the *Backyardigans* before bedtime. It is very possible that as parents, we are confusing our children's needs from their wants. There are many things in culture today that we would ascribe as needs that just a few years ago were luxuries. Things like air-conditioning, microwaves, refrigerators, cell phones, cars, televisions, toasters, Amazon, carpet, electricity, running water, flushable toilets, etc. The reality is that many people in our world don't have these things. Yet the consumption narrative has renamed these as needs, not wants. Dr. Christian Smith and his team found that "this generation of emerging adults might not merely be neglecting the distinction between need and want, they might, more tragically, never have learned this critical difference in the first place."

While this consumer mindset has more than likely been formed through unintentional efforts and through cultural pursuits, we are faced with the reality that *want* always overcomes *should*. So we must be intentional in our efforts to cultivate our children's wants. Jesus's command to follow Him is a command to align our wants and longings with His wants, to desire what God desires, to hunger and thirst after God, and to crave a world where He is all in all.

These young people are being taken captive to the narrative of consumerism. According to Sen. Ben Sasse in his book, *The Vanishing American Adult*:

> The more affluent the society, the more likely young people will experience an extended drift toward adulthood. Wealthy societies, for reasons largely well-intentioned but now producing unintended consequences, are making it easier for their teens to avoid the rigors and responsibilities of becoming a grown-up.

Truthfully, I spend my days around people of affluence. These are people who don't have a problem going out to eat, taking great vacations, or having a night out on the town. I'm a blessed man with a wonderful family and a good job, but to be honest, it scares me a bit. There are some factual truths about affluence that can be

a bit disheartening, and it seems like they are connected.
Now I don't want to come across as this ridiculous guy saying, people have it so bad," but there are concerns when raising affluent children that should be addressed.

In his book *How Children Succeed*, Paul Tough pointed out that "wealthy parents today are more likely than others to be emotionally distant from their children while at the same time insisting on high levels of achievement." He goes on to highlight some significant statistics:

- Affluent students are found to use alcohol, cigarettes, marijuana, and harder illegal drugs more than low-income teens. Thirty-five percent of suburban girls have tried all four, compared to 15 percent of inner-city girls.
- Wealthier girls reported elevated rates of depression (22 percent).

A possible causation of all of this would be the pressure these children have to overachieve while having an emotionally distant relationship with their parents. So what should we do?

Practical tip. Travel. Take your children to a place very different from the one you know. Allow your children/youth group/students to have diverse experiences that stretch and grow them. The obvious opportunity here is the overseas Third World country trip, but it doesn't have to be so far. About eight years ago, a youth minister and I spent the night in downtown Austin, Texas. We wanted to know what it was like to be homeless. I know one night on the street is a rather weak attempt to experience homelessness, but it was enough to open my eyes to a new world. Since then, this youth minister has taken kids with him to experience the same thing.

Practical tip. Jesus valued relationships. We need to be more intentional with our relationships. I had a coworker named Grey Powell that might have been one of the best at building relationships with kids. Grey has spent his career as either a youth minister, teacher, or coach for the past few decades and I would argue has mastered the art of relationship building. One of his strategies is to remain engaged in their spaces. So he is very intentional with immersing himself in their culture to understand their movies, media, language, and their loves. He believes no matter how old he is (he's actually a grandpa now and still killing it at relationships with sixteen-year-olds) that he can remain attune to their worlds.

Practical tip. We must reevaluate our expectations of our children. Recently, I helped honor kids that had contributed to the world. When I asked for nominations, I was surprised at the submissions. The type of submissions I received really led me to see the lack of expectations we have for our children. Things like my daughter raised money so she could go to a weeklong summer camp. Or my son went on a mission trip with his youth group to Honduras. These aren't bad things, but the children we recognized are part of a group of kids that are truly bearing God's image in powerful ways. Raising the expectations of our children to be active contributors to society again by bearing the image of God in our world is crucial to their faith formation.

If we expect the next generation to become contributors to society, we must be intentional in our cultivation tactics. Contributors are not accidentally created:

1. Write down the skill sets you want to see in your child, youth group, school, etc.
2. Start early. Even two-year-olds can learn skills like responsibility by picking up their rooms, putting dirty clothes in the hamper, and getting ready for bath time.
3. Develop an intentional plan to teach, remind, form, and guide these skills into your students.
4. Have adult contributors mentor students. Discipleship is a key aspect of developing contributors.
5. Provide them opportunities to practice and fail. Let's go back to an apprenticeship model where students are put into *action moments* that push them. Let them fail safely in an environment of a loving community.
6. Hold them accountable to the skill set. When they don't show responsibility, hold them accountable to that. Don't

solve problems for them; hold them accountable by making them critically think through situations before you offer suggestions or advice.

CHAPTER 3

Living in a Broken Culture of Parenting

> There is no normal life that is free of pain. It's the very wrestling with our problems that can be the impetus for our growth.
>
> —Mr. Rogers

This emerging group of kids desires to be impactful and make meaning in their world. It is evident that they care about things like social justice, world issues, and fairness for humanity. However, it is interesting that they (even Christians in Generation Z) are not more actively engaged in these issues. Let's take a look at why this might be.

I can't say I was thrilled about moving to Oklahoma as I was living in a pretty great city in Austin, Texas. I was excited about my new role as a K-12 superintendent, and I was excited to meet a new group of people, but I can't say I was thrilled about living in Oklahoma. I didn't know much about Oklahoma except for the fact that they despised the Texas Longhorns. Growing up in Austin, Texas, this was an issue. I was excited about one thing though and that was the Oklahoma Thunder, and it helped that at that time, they had a Texas Longhorn player named Kevin Durant. I love basketball and was excited to live in a city with a professional basketball team.

I'll never forget the first game I went to, and I was shocked at what they did prior to tip-off. You non-Oklahomans won't believe this but the Thunder franchise actually does a prayer before every

RAISING CONTRIBUTORS
IN A CULTURE OF CONSUMERISM AND SKEPTICISM

basketball game. One of the best surprises in our move to Oklahoma was the friendly Christian culture in which we live. Prayer seems to be a normal part of life here, obviously within the church, but in everyday life as well. For the past four years, we have attended the Oklahoma Governor's Prayer Breakfast. For the past eight years, I have attended the mayor's prayer breakfast for my city. It's a common occurrence to go to lunch with someone for the first time and they ask to say a prayer before the meal. Oklahoman's pray.

As Christians, our prayers tend to have the same consistent themes. I remember being in college and sitting in the steep balcony of a green-carpeted Baptist Church when the pastor started to bring his message to a close and the soft piano keys began to play faintly in the background as he prayed. You know this moment, and many of you have distinct memories of this liturgical church practice. He began to talk about the cross and what it means for our sinful humanity. He then began to proceed and ask those in attendance who wanted to be saved to raise their hands, and he would pray a prayer of salvation over them. This Baptist tradition is not the one I grew up in, but this type of *altar call* is one many of us experience.

I grew up within the churches of Christ and remember hearing my preacher dad quote at the end of every sermon, "If you would like to be baptized for the remission of your sins, please come as we stand and sing." Most Christian church experiences have this moment within their church worship. In fact, much of our church liturgies are appropriately aligned with the redemptive understanding of God saving us from our sinful nature. It is a rare opportunity in my church experience to hear a prayer that does not thank our God for sending His Son to save us from our sins or thankful for His grace in a broken and fallen world.

I have always felt that the best way to understand a group's central theology was to listen to the way they pray. What are the things they pray about? What are the themes in the prayers that we continually hear? So for the past year, I have been intentional with listening to the prayers of my community. From Sunday morning worship, lunch with professionals, our city's prayer breakfast, to the Oklahoma Thunder basketball games, I listened and took notes. This probably doesn't surprise you, but here are the themes or words that were consistently used in the prayers:

- Thankfulness
- Grace
- Mercy
- Forgiveness of sins
- Sick people
- Government
- Love
- Jesus's sacrifice

I think this list of words sums up a limited theology in which we see lived out among Christians but also I think is connected to a distinct parenting phenomenon in our culture. Looking at these words, I am convinced that we have a poor theology that centralizes around Genesis chapter 3.

This theology goes something like this. God created the world. He created man and put him in the garden. While in the garden, Adam was tempted by Eve and ate an apple from the tree of knowledge of good and evil, and sin entered the world. Now, man is fallen and broken, and we have been separated from God. We are living in a broken world consumed by sin. Fortunately, Jesus came to this world to save us from this brokenness. He died and rose again so that one day we may have eternal life with Him. Nothing about this theology is wrong or even counter textual, but it is a gospel centered around the brokenness of our world.

When your theology stems from Genesis 3, a driving parental value is protection

You want to protect your children from the brokenness and sin in the world. You want to do everything you can to make sure their life is easy and free from adversity. As we look back over the past fifty

RAISING CONTRIBUTORS
IN A CULTURE OF CONSUMERISM AND SKEPTICISM

years, we can see some interesting landmarks between culture and the protection phenomenon seen in parenting:

- 1978–1985: Every state adopted a car seat law
- 1980: Abduction of Adam Walsh
- 1980s: A heightened concern for children's self-esteem and the protection of competition came with it
- 1983: Concern for lack of school work with the famous publication, "A Nation at Risk"
- 1984: The playdate emerged
- 1990: Helicopter parenting. While this phrase took off in the 90s, Dr. Lythcott-Haims argued that from 1946–1964, the baby boom generation was the first parenting generation to receive this title. This generation was seventy-six million strong, and until their children, they were the largest generation ever. This generation changed parenting in the US forever. They were the tipping point. Boomer's parents were emotionally distant, so boomers were overwhelmingly emotionally present.
- 1994: First bicycle helmet was invented
- 2000: The American Academy of Pediatrics released a policy prohibiting specialization in sports
- 2014: Remote mini brake for a bicycle was invented so a parent can brake remotely

As seen earlier, the differences between earlier generations and generations today are striking. Over time, parents have wanted to create a better world for their children than the one they grew up in. With pure intentions, our overprotection began to create a climate that is now stunting our children's ability to develop and grow. This has major ramifications on their spirituality. I greatly value the work of Dr. Tim Elmore and his dedication to the younger generations. His books *Artificial Maturity* and *Marching Off the Map* are two key books in discussing younger generations. One of the charts he has published to discuss the needs of our children is called childhood messages vs. adolescent messages.

Childhood Messages	*Adolescent Messages*
1. You are loved.	1. Life is difficult.
2. You are unique.	2. You are not in control.
3. You have gifts.	3. You are not that important.
4. You are safe.	4. You are going to die.
5. You are valuable.	5. Your life is not about you.

This chart indicates that there are essential messages that we must teach our children at an early age. We know that if children get the adolescent messages too early, it will cause trauma in their lives. We see this a lot in children who grow up in difficult homes—children that experience abuse, death of a loved one, abandonment, and all the horrific life events some children must face far too early in life. However, on the flip side, if we protect our children from the adolescent messages too late, trauma may occur. A question I typically get about this chart when I show this to groups is, at what age do they need to start getting adolescent messages? I believe by age twelve they really need to start hearing these messages.

Now we should use good sense because it wouldn't be appropriate to sit our twelve-year-olds down and let them know they will all be dying. Could you imagine? "Okay, son, now that you have turned twelve, I want you to know that you're not very important, and you're going to die!" Of course we wouldn't do this. However, these are the messages that they need to be taught about life as they mature. The best way to teach adolescent messages is by letting life happen to them. As we know, unfortunately, we are living within a parenting context that is adamant about protecting their children from adversity.

I remember in ninth grade I transitioned into a high school that had significantly higher academic expectations than the one I had come from. So it was in my freshman year of high school that I had to actually write a research paper for the first time. And the most bizarre aspect was that it was a paper for geometry. (Figure that out!)

RAISING CONTRIBUTORS IN A CULTURE OF CONSUMERISM AND SKEPTICISM

The assignment was to build a bridge with raw spaghetti noodles using only Elmer's glue. Then once we built the bridge, we had to write a lengthy paper about different kinds of bridges.

It was also around this time that we got a computer in my home. This computer actually had paper where you had to tear off the edges, remember that? I don't think we had the internet, or if we did, I didn't really know how to use it; but we did have this encyclopedia floppy disk that I could use for research. Well, I used it, and according to my school administrators, I used it too much. My teacher gave my paper to the principal, and pretty soon, I was being called to the office. Now I was not a perfect kid but in all my years in education, I had never been sent to the office for a discipline matter. But here I am, a new kid, in a new school, in my first year, being called to the principal's office.

As I sat in the principal's office scared to death, he asked if I had plagiarized. He could tell I was confused, so he began to define and explain plagiarism. I soon confessed my transgression, and Mr. Bush looked at me and said, "Well, you will receive a zero on this assignment, and we are going to have to place you on academic probation."

He then went on to spend about thirty minutes discussing the strategies he used to write papers and to keep his thoughts and his sources separate. Interestingly, as I wrote my dissertation for my doctoral degree and had hundreds of sources, I remembered the advice of Mr. Bush who shaped me at that moment. I tell this story to ask this question: what do you think my parents did when I got home? The answer: nothing; they did absolutely nothing except support what Mr. Bush said. Fast forward to 2019 and let me explain to you how that conversation looks with a parent now because they feel the need to protect their kids from hardship.

BRANDON. Mom you won't believe this. Mr. Bush and Mrs. Foust said I cheated on my paper and are giving me a zero, and now I'm on academic probation.
MOM. What?! You have got to be kidding! Did they prove that you were cheating?

BRANDON. No they just assumed it because I used big words, but Mom, I used a thesaurus.
MOM. I am emailing Mr. Bush now…

> Email:
> Subject: Need Some Answers!
>
> David,
>
>   I called your cell five times with no answer this evening, so I decided to email you. Brandon came home today telling me of your accusations, and I would like some answers as soon as possible. First, what evidence do you have that he actually plagiarized? We are new to this school, and it's obvious you do not know us, but my son has never been in trouble, and for whatever reason, you have decided to target my son. Why? Can you answer that? Second, my son has never been in trouble, and I think the punishment you gave is completely inappropriate. I know for a fact because Brandon told me that other kids were cheating in this class. What happened to them? I am told nothing happened to them! How is that fair? A zero will negatively impact my son's grades, and we must get him into college. How will we explain this? Also, will this academic probation go on his record, and will this keep him from getting into college or a college scholarship? I feel like you are sabotaging any chance my son has in the future.
>
>   Sincerely,
>   Brandon's mom

RAISING CONTRIBUTORS
IN A CULTURE OF CONSUMERISM AND SKEPTICISM

Some of you who read that email and think, *No way. No way would someone send an email like this.* Others who are reading this may be thinking, *Well, the email I sent was much tamer than that, but I really don't think my son cheated.* Those of you who are educators or youth workers have received an email like this, and your anxiety is on the rise. Sorry about that!

All I can say is this: I am so thankful that my parents allowed me to get zeros and be put on academic probation. Even if I hadn't really cheated, this would have been an adolescent message that needed to be taught. I learned it under the safest of circumstances. When we spend our parenting years protecting our children from adolescent messages, we are literally stunting their human development. And if we are stunting human development, what do you think happens to their faith development? It's no wonder our children can't handle the realities of life when they have never been allowed to experience them.

Paul Tough, author of *How Children Succeed*, wrote, "Interestingly we [parents] are pushing for high achievement yet, shielding from experiences that create growth." This line hits the nail on the head for me. Through my education, my time coaching and teaching, and my work as a leader, this line continues to ring true.

David Kinnaman has this to say about parents in his book, *Gen Z*:

> In assessing the parenting approach of Gen Z's mostly Gen X parents, observers seem to fall into one of two camps. In one are those who believe Gen Z's caregivers are of the "helicopter" variety: overprotective, hyper-managing and fearful. On the other hand, there are those who suggest just the opposite: that most Gen X parents are, in fact, *under*protective because they are so keen to avoid the helicopter label. The truth, however, may be a combination of both extremes, a parenting dichotomy: overprotective in some ways and underprotective in others (especially in

digital spaces). The apostle James warns against being "double-minded" because wavering and vacillation make a person (or parent) unstable. Could that be what's going on here?

Part of this tension found in the parenting climate stems from a fear-based pressure of society at large. Hanna Rosin in a 2014 article from *The Atlantic* argued, "Actions that would have been considered paranoid in the '70s—walking third-graders to school, forbidding your kid to play ball in the street, going down the slide with your child in your lap—are now routine. In fact, they are the markers of good, responsible parenting."

Do you remember the story of the woman being sued for allowing her nine-year-old daughter to play alone at a playground? It was a mother in South Carolina who worked at McDonald's, and while at work, she allowed her daughter to play at a popular public playground. I find this story eye-opening on many levels but especially under the light of the work of Dr. Roger Hart, a professor and researcher at City University of New York. He has spent his life working to understand child development.

Dr. Hart's work has fascinated me for several years, and I have found one of his studies most interesting. The study actually began as his doctoral dissertation in 1972 when he moved to a small town. The original study focused on all children in this town under the age of twelve and followed closely for two years. The study examined these primary things: how they use the town, what places were valued, and who they used the places with. Hart discovered between second and third grade, for instance, the children's *free range*—the distance they were allowed to travel away from home without checking in first—tended to expand significantly because they were permitted to ride bikes alone to a friend's house or to a ball field.

By fifth grade, the boys especially gained a *dramatic, new freedom*. To the children, each little addition to their free range—being allowed to cross a paved road or go to the center of town—was a sign of growing up. The kids took special pride in *knowing how to get places* and in finding shortcuts that adults wouldn't normally use.

Based on the new freedoms they received from their parents, they found a sense of maturing or new responsibility.

This is actually an interesting piece that is slipping away from growing up today. It appears we have lost anything in culture to help guide our children into adulthood. At one point in history, we had clear markers for adulthood. For example, the life of a knight shows the systematic and ceremonial aspect of a boy becoming a man. We simply have lost systematic moments of guiding our kids from youth to adulthood.

Fascinatingly, Dr. Hart went back to this same town and wanted to understand and reexamine the children in 2014. He went back to this town to reconnect with the kids he had interviewed in the 70s to see how they were raising their children. What was similar and what was different? In an interview, Dr. Hart told Hanna of *The Atlantic*, "There's a fear' among the parents, 'an exaggeration of the dangers, a loss of trust that isn't totally clearly explainable." Children used to gradually take on responsibilities year by year. They crossed the road, went to the store; eventually, some of them got small neighborhood jobs. Their pride was wrapped up in competence and independence, which grew as they tried and mastered activities they hadn't known how to do the previous year.

But these days, middle-class children, at least, skip these milestones. They spend a lot of time in the company of adults, so they can talk and think like them, but they never build up the confidence to be truly independent and self-reliant. We live in a parenting culture driven by fear, but we have significant data telling us that life is actually safer now than it was back then. You wouldn't know it by turning on the news because they need ratings and murder seems to get our attention, but did you know that as of 2014, there is a 0.01 percent chance your child will be abducted?

Regardless, for the most part, we protect, we advocate, and we fight for our kids' happiness at all costs even though our world is safer now than ever before.

Historical Parenting Spectrum

1970s and Prior to	*Today's Perception*
Free-range parenting	Negligence
Winners and losers	Success over failure
Trust and development	Paranoid and protective
Encouraging hobbies	Forcing hobbies
Expected to contribute	Expected to be happy

I know as a parent that it feels natural to protect our kids from all the sin and brokenness out there. However, no matter how much we try to protect, we must always remember that the snake is out there trying to get to our kids. Even the beautiful garden of Eden had a snake roaming around trying to deceive the first humans working the garden. The snake successfully led man down a pathway of consumption and off the path to contribution.

Practical tip. Parents, make your child do something hard. Make them apologize to an adult or ask a teacher about a problem face-to-face. Teachers, when that student comes to you about a problem, recognize that they are doing a hard thing and treat them with respect. Youth leaders, find ways in your youth group to rally around the broken in your church. Allow them to experience suffering with their peers, and create a safe environment for them to be open and honest.

While we shelter our kids with our best intentions, it leads to the formation of a fixed mindset in them. A person with a fixed mindset will not grow, learn, or try new things. These are the people that say can't, won't, and quit easily. They avoid failure and tend to be complacent. We can teach them to say can, will, and to persevere.

Practical tip. For kids to be able to deal with life's difficulties and obstacles, they must develop a growth mindset. Researcher Dr. Carol Dweck encourages leaders, teachers, and parents to develop growth mindsets in their children. It's a complex theory that can be broken down into two simple thoughts. Growth mindset means that your ability to learn is not fixed, and it can change with effort. Let's encourage our children to learn and grow within their own personal

RAISING CONTRIBUTORS
IN A CULTURE OF CONSUMERISM AND SKEPTICISM

interests. Remember, not all kids will be mathematicians, and that's okay, but they will love something. Encourage growth in those loves.

An important second aspect of a growth mindset is that failure is not a permanent condition. In other words, failure is temporary and should be used as an opportunity to grow. An individual with a growth mindset owns failure. When our children make mistakes, whether it involves disciplinary action or just a bad grade, be careful how you handle it and address it. When your child makes a mistake, maybe your response should be, "I'm glad I know about this because we can use this opportunity to grow."

Research shows that children who don't learn how to deal with failure go on to struggle with relationship development as adults. We must mold our kids into the adults they deserve to be. We can do that now by standing by their side as they fail, succeed, and learn how to recover and grow from both.

We've been entrusted with a lot. We're not just responsible for the first eighteen years of our children's lives. The way we teach them today will mold their decision-making and problem-solving skills for their adult lives as well. It may be harder today, but it will make all of us better in the long run.

Practical tip. Cultivate hard things. Angela Duckworth, the leading researcher of *Grit*, has a rule in her house that everyone must follow. It's called the Do Hard Things Rule. Here is the framework:

1. Everyone has to do a hard thing that takes deliberate practice.
2. You can't quit until the tuition payment is finished or the season is over.
3. You can't quit until you choose another hard thing to do next.

I like this rule and concept because it helps develop contributors. It encourages "doing hard things" while allowing children to explore various passions. Our children must learn through trial and error how they can contribute before they will begin to leave consumption behind.

We have another problem with a theology centered around protecting our kids from a broken and sinful world.

When your theology stems from Genesis 3, a driving parental value is advocacy

We tend to view advocacy as a good word in parenting terms. Right? I am my child's biggest advocate. I am my child's biggest supporter. I am afraid, though, that the seesaw of advocacy and accountability is off balance. Our desire to be our child's advocate is overpowering our need to hold our children accountable.

This book is somewhat therapeutic for me as I have recently transitioned out of the most difficult job I have had in my life, superintendent of a pre-K-12 private Christian school in the midst of the current parenting climate clinically known as *sucky*. I have never admitted this publicly to anyone other than my wife, so a book seems to be the best way to do so, but in my tenure, I was diagnosed with levels of manic anxiety.

From all practical and outward appearances, my time as a head of school was successful. First, I had an amazing board and team of people around me to do life with. We grew enrollment by 123 percent, increased the annual budget by two million, baptized around seventy students, and increased diversity within the student body. There were many things we were able to accomplish, but the climate of parenting in our culture today is something that surprised me, and quite honestly, I wasn't prepared for.

In her book *How to Raise An Adult*, Julie Lythcott-Haims highlighted this quote from Dr. Tim Waldon, a school administrator from Massachusetts:

> I've been a school administrator since 1998, and have had to call a lot of parents with bad news. I might say 'Your kid has been cutting class; we found him on Route 1 at Burger King. As a result, here is the consequence.' In 1998, most of the time I could get a supportive response like,

RAISING CONTRIBUTORS
IN A CULTURE OF CONSUMERISM AND SKEPTICISM

> 'That's bad. We want to work with the school to make this right.' But nowadays when I call home, I hear the parents go through the process of questioning my authority and my judgment. 'Why are you doing this Dr. Waldon? Surely you are wrong.'

My experiences mimic Dr. Waldon's because it felt as if we had to present a court case in front of a parent every time a child was in trouble because it is the parents' responsibility to advocate for their child at all costs.

You may have seen some researchers using the term *lawnmower* parenting because now they will run over anyone in their children's way. A study from the University of Tennessee at Chattanooga found that students with *hovering* or *helicopter* parents were more likely to take medication for anxiety, depression, or both. In a parenting seminar I helped create alongside my good friend Dr. Sada Knowles, we created a unit on helping parents understand the potential consequences to making advocacy a key tenet of parenting. When you step back and look at both historical and current parenting research, it's evident that being your child's advocate is not a helpful hat to wear when trying to develop them.

Regardless, many parents in our culture won't hear this. I remember sitting in the seminar while a parent raised their hand asking Dr. Knowles, "But what if your child is being treated unfairly? Isn't that an appropriate time to advocate?" Correct answer: *nope*. Our children will learn more about life in the unfair moments than if we attempt to structure their lives in a fair world that quite honestly does not exist.

I am new to the parenting role and admittedly not a professional parenter. In fact, I am learning as I go, but fortunately, due to my work, I have had the unique experience to watch a lot of good parenting and bad parenting up close and personal. I hope to say that I had the wisdom to learn from watching these experiences play out. There was a moment in my educational career when I had a series of parents upset about how a particular coach handled the selection of the team captains in a particular sport. A certain senior player was not selected as captain and therefore another child was selected. The frustration stemmed from the fact that the player who did not get the captain position had high character, longevity with the program, dedication to the team, and all the other traits desired for a team captain.

Even though I was surprised and disappointed in the decision of this coach, I was baffled by one thing—this particular player's parents never contacted me. A plethora of other parents jumped on the advocacy bandwagon because this was a major injustice and completely not fair! The tensions were high, and I ended up calling this player's father because we were close friends. That conversation looked like this:

ME. Hey, I have some folks frustrated about the captain selections, and by all accounts, it appears your child deserved a spot. Can you tell me how you feel?
DAD. Yeah, we think our child should have been a captain. Our kid has given everything to that team and has been a part of this community since elementary school. My wife and I can't figure out what is going on.
ME. Well, why haven't you called me?
DAD: My wife and I decided we aren't going to do anything about it except allow this to teach our child a lesson. It's our belief that life is not fair and that our child will have these moments many more times in her adult life. We feel it is better for her to learn a lesson like this while we are around her, so we can help her navigate this. So in many ways, we are grateful this opportunity happened.
ME. Wow, I have been in this position for a few years, and I am grateful to have a conversation like this. Thank you for deciding to parent your child.

I will never forget this moment, and it was parents like this that made my job wonderful because it allowed me the unique opportunity to see parenting at its finest. These unfair moments in childhood are such good ways to learn life's lessons. As I think back on my childhood, I had multiple moments like this. One of the most memorable moments involved little league baseball.

You see, I should have made the fourth-grade baseball all-star team! I played for the Mets and proudly wore yellow and white. I was clearly the best player on the team and had been playing since kindergarten. So the years of experience had set the stage for this being my year of greatness.

This was also the year that I had been trained by a Major League pitcher. At that time, Nathan Minchey was a pitcher for the Boston Red Sox, and he grew up at the same church as me. I remember as a kid my dad waking me up at night every time Nathan took the mound, and we would huddle around the TV just to watch. Nathan gave me personal pitching lessons in his off-season. I was good! So when the season was over and we were at the closing ceremonies, I knew my name would be called for the all-star team. But it wasn't! The head coach's son's name was called. My dad was just the assistant coach.

I vividly remember being so mad at my dad! How could he not stand up for me in the coaches' meeting and make sure I got on the all-star team? It was simply an injustice. I can remember the anger I felt, and I can remember how mad I was that my parents decided to do nothing to help me get on that team! Funny to consider how my parents might have handled this situation today under the current parenting strategies. My mother probably would have written an email like this:

> Subject: Grievance with All-Star Team Selection
>
> Dear Pflugerville Little League
> Board of Directors,
>
> I am writing to you to make you aware of the idiotic decision not to allow my son to be on the fourth-grade all-star team. I have attached to

this email my son's statistics and a video recording that covers my son's highlights throughout the course of the season. After reviewing my documentation, it will appear evident to you that favoritism was shown to the head coach's son and that this has impacted my son's psyche. I also want to make you aware that because of your blatant decision to shun my child from the all-star team, he has developed post-traumatic stress disorder (PTSD). By allowing the coach's son to remain on the team, you are conspiring with the coach, and I will make certain that other parents know about this through Facebook, Instagram, and local news outlets. Other parents need to know how you willingly disregard quality athletes in your league and publicly promote favoritism and nepotism. I expect to hear back from the board on their decision to allow my son to be on the team, and if the answer is no, you will be hearing from our attorney.

Sincerely,
Brandon's supportive mother

Well fortunately, I did not have a mom that would write such an email. As an adult, I am so thankful for the sanity of my parents. As I look back on this situation, I'm so thankful for the way my parents handled it. Recently, during my research, I began processing what I learned from this experience and what I would have learned if my parents had fought to get me on that team.

RAISING CONTRIBUTORS IN A CULTURE OF CONSUMERISM AND SKEPTICISM

If my parents had complained,	*Because they didn't complain,*
I would have learned my parents loved me.	I learned a lot later how much more they loved me because they didn't complain.
I would have learned that you can manipulate the system.	I learned life is not fair.
I would have learned that I can get my way by how I manipulate my parents.	I learned to work harder and improve.
I would have learned that my parents will fight my battles for me.	I learned to suck it up (grit).

If you think I am being dramatic about parenting in this current generation, how's this? I wrote this story about my baseball experience in a blog for my school community. My point was very similar in the context of that blog, and the day I posted it, I got this email overnight from a parent of a student at my school:

Mr. Tatum,

Nice article although I disagree on many points.

I bet your baseball league had a system that actually allowed the best players to play no matter what the "coaches" wanted, which is a far cry from our system today. Where the only 9th grade player that actually played was a coach's son and where even when we led the starters weren't pulled from the game to allow other players to play cause the coaches son could rack up stats.

> Your "points" are incorrect. What about parents standing up to a wrong system? What about kids seeing their parents stand up to authority that they are paying their salaries for? What about parents that stand up for systems that reward a grade level and not playing level? I bet you weren't even good at baseball.
>
> Your article is not accurate for sports where the weak make Junior Varsity and the strong don't get to try out and seven kids get cut from the team but whatever it takes to make you feel like you're doing the right thing.
>
> Sorry but you miss the mark on what is accurate and right in my opinion and I will stand up to you or any authority that claims this nonsense.
>
> Sincerely,
> Your biggest supporter

That is just a small portion of the email, but believe it or not, I actually received an apology from this parent after they sent this and acknowledged that their complaints were not accurate. Regardless, that was a fun email to wake up to the next morning. Anyways, my point was that I learned a lot more about real life by not being on that all-star team than by being on the team.

Practical tip. Find a friend that you trust and respect and ask them to keep you accountable to keeping a proper perspective of advocacy versus accountability for your child. Think back to my chart on what I learned about life by my parents not advocating for me. Next time you want to put on an advocacy hat, think to yourself, *What will my child learn from this life experience?*

The final problem with a theology centered around protecting our kids from a broken and sinful world is this…

RAISING CONTRIBUTORS
IN A CULTURE OF CONSUMERISM AND SKEPTICISM

When your theology stems from Genesis 3, a driving parental value is happiness

I was a couple of years into my role as superintendent dealing with the nuances of the job and navigating the parental landscape. Frustrated at times but able to keep a clear head through it all, I remember this one distinct moment that changed the tenor of my outlook on parenting, and in many aspects, my outlook on life. A husband and a wife, parents of middle schoolers, set up a meeting with me and my principal one morning at 8:00 a.m. This day, like many others, was full of various meetings, so this was just the first of several. Quickly into this first meeting, I knew it would not be a typical meeting nor was I prepared for what I was about to hear.

The meeting started with something like this from the father: "Well, this weekend, we sat our kids down and told them that I was going to die soon." This father had been diagnosed with cancer, and it was overtaking his body.

"There have been moments over the past year and a half where we have had similar conversations because we thought we were nearing the end of my life, but God has graciously allowed me to see more life. I say that because my kids think it was just another time Dad said he was going to die, but sadly, all reports indicate my death is near."

The meeting then centered around what would happen after his death and what schooling would look like for his kids upon his passing. I literally walked out of that office immediately into a different office to meet with another family. That conversation went something like this: "Mr. Tatum, we have a significant issue with our child's stats in the sport Sally is playing. We went to MaxPreps online to see the team statistics and noticed major discrepancies between our family stats and the coaches' stats. In fact, they are so obviously wrong it appears your coach is attempting to sabotage my child's chances at college athletics."

Insert eyeroll emoji here. I was somewhat more prepared for this ridiculous conversation than I was at my prior meeting because this family felt the need to share it with some board members prior to them setting up a meeting with me.

Found in the dissonance between these two experiences highlights a fascinating phenomenon in parenting today. A parent's conflict between their children being happy versus their children learning to become functional and healthy adults. Pretty quickly, I began saying these types of things to my team: "We won't be able to spiritually form these children if they can't first function in life" or "Let's just raise functional adults and then we can begin forming their spiritual beliefs."

You might be wondering what type of functionality I am talking about. How's this for a quick list:

- Remember to put shoes on before you go to school.
- Getting out of bed to come to school
- Showering
- Putting your homework in your backpack

These may seem ridiculous or over the top, but go ask an educator if what I am saying resonates with them. If you don't believe me, pick up the phone and call a teacher or a principal and see if I am just making this stuff up. We are not raising functional adults today. Dr. Leonard Sax calls this the *collapse of parenting*. In his book, he illustrates this quite effectively. He said:

> As recently as 1994 it was rare for any individual under the age of 20 to be diagnosed as bipolar. But by 2003, in the United States, it was becoming common. There was a fourfold increase in the diagnosis of bipolar disorder among American children and teenagers just between 1994 and 2003. In other words, for every one kid diagnosed with bipolar disorder in 1994, 40 kids were diagnosed in 2003. And most of the new diagnoses were for American children under the age of 15.

RAISING CONTRIBUTORS IN A CULTURE OF CONSUMERISM AND SKEPTICISM

After more research and analysis of bipolar diagnosis in other countries, it is evident that these were misdiagnosed by doctors, and it was easier to give a parent a diagnosis than to tell them they needed a different parenting strategy. Dr. Sax furthered this discussion by highlighting the work of Dr. Elizzabeth Roberts, "Psychiatrists are now misdiagnosing and overmedicating children for ordinary defiance and misbehavior. The temper tantrums of belligerent children are increasingly being characterized as psychiatric illnesses."

Another takeaway I had from the back-to-back meetings with parents was that our parental values are misaligned and disconnected from the role of parenting. So what is the role of parenting? Dr. Lythcott-Haims took a sarcastic tone when she articulated the role of parenting:

> Our job is to monitor our kids' academic tasks and progress, schedule and supervise their activities, shuttle them everywhere, and offer an outpouring of praise along the way. Our kids' accomplishments are the measure of our own success and worth; that college bumper sticker on the rear of our car can be as much about our own sense of accomplishment as our kids.

From a Christian perspective, parents are called to be the number one faith influencer in their child's life as indicated in Deuteronomy 6. Another crucial role in parenting is to lead our children into successful adulthood. I will let you define success as you see fit, but for the purposes of this book, I define success as someone who understands the rules of life, has mastered certain character traits that help them positively navigate relationships and work, and can handle the average adversity that life throws at them.

Dr. Tim Elmore, an author, national speaker, and teen researcher, has put some interesting information together about raising this current generation of kids. He says that our children's world is full of speed, convenience, entertainment, nurture, and entitlement. What are the consequences of these things? He went on to highlight

- if our children's world is full of *speed*, they will view *slow* as bad;
- if our children's world is full of *convenience*, they will view *hard* as bad;
- if our children's world is full of *entertainment*, they will view *boring* as bad;
- if our children's world is full of *nurture*, they will view *risk* as bad; and
- if our children's world is full of *entitlement*, they will view *labor* as bad.

Think about this for a second. What are the implications for our children? How do they view slow, hard, boring, risk, and labor? As an adult, I often have to deal with slow, hard, boring, risk, and labor. If I have a hard time in my marriage, how do I respond? If work is boring for a period, how do I respond? How can I function as a follower of Jesus if adversity is bad?

We know that this must be a balancing act because life is also full of speed, convenience, entertainment, nurturing, and entitlement. We also know that these things are not inherently bad. The key is knowing when the right opportunities arise to teach each of these. For many of us, raising a child can be overly centered around activities like sports, camps, playdates, and the usually wonderful activities that make childhood great. As a parent, my fear is that I'll become so consumed with the normal activities of my children's social life that I will be less intentional with the long-lasting skills needed to develop a contributor.

We also see something interesting about humanity as it relates to Genesis 3. We see humanity as passive beings overcome by the desire to want more and consume. Allowing students to be consumers creates a culture of passivity. Passivity seems to be a word being used a lot right now in relation to cultural outcomes, particularly those related to adolescents. In the book *Raising a Modern-Day Knight*,

RAISING CONTRIBUTORS IN A CULTURE OF CONSUMERISM AND SKEPTICISM

Robert Lewis suggested four goals for raising boys in the context of American culture. He argued they must understand how to lead courageously, accept responsibility, reject passivity, and expect a greater reward.

Passivity is a common story that I often hear from families. A story of fear that their children are turning into passive beings through consumption and addiction to their devices, or as Senator Sasse says, "zombie like."

Adam and Eve were in the garden as the serpent approached them with the proposition to eat the fruit and they will *be like God*. Adam had the opportunity to say no and continue his contribution efforts of tending to the garden. In fact, you fully expect Adam to come running with a garden hoe, cut off the serpent's head, and end this heinous approach of evil. But confronted with his social and spiritual responsibilities, Adam becomes, of all things, passive.

Practical tip. Think about the list Dr. Elmore provides and think through how you can be intentional in helping your child counteract the lessons their world is teaching them.

If our children's world is full of *speed*, they will view *slow* as bad.

If our children's world is full of *convenience*, they will view *hard* as bad.

If our children's world is full of *entertainment*, they will view *boring* as bad.

If our children's world is full of *nurture*, they will view *risk* as bad.

If our children's world is full of *entitlement*, they will view *labor* as bad.

CHAPTER 4

A More Hopeful Parenting Culture

As human beings, our job in life is to help people realize how rare and valuable each one of us really is, that each of us has something that no one else has—or ever will have—something inside that is unique to all time. It's our job to encourage each other to discover that uniqueness and to provide ways of developing its expression.

—Mr. Rogers

Let's shift here and think about a new way to approach our parenting theology, and as we do this, let's go back to the farm. I came across an interesting article written by Rudy Taylor who gives an assessment of growing up on a farm:

> While attending a job fair last week where Taylor Newspapers manned a booth, I met lots of job seekers. Some brought resumes. Others just moseyed by, picked up the free stuff on our table and asked a few questions. But one young woman created a memory for me. She was a senior in high school, seeking summer employment before starting at a community college in the fall.
> "Are you hiring?" she asked.

We said probably not, but we're always looking for good resources, such as part-time photographers and writers.

"We'd be happy to take your resume," I told her.

Then she said something that stuck with me.

"I'm afraid my resume wouldn't be too impressive," she said. "I've spent all my life working on my parents' farm. I go to school in the daytime and do chores in the morning and at night."

Whoa.

I told her to go home and create a resume, and write down exactly what she had told me.

As a farm girl, one who has driven a tractor since she was 12, one who has cleaned out barns, scooped grain until her back arched, fed chickens, pigs, cattle and goats—this girl knows the meaning of work. She knows about dependability and getting jobs done on time. The morning school bus won't wait until a farm kid finishes those chores. They'll be done on time or the young student will miss that all-important ride. A young person, who has put up hay, helped her dad and mother in the farrowing house or candled eggs has something more than words to jot on a resume.

Farm kids don't need to take art appreciation classes in school. They witness picturesque landscapes, sunrises and changes in seasons as they grow up. They ride horses, drive four-wheelers and neatly stack big bales at the edge of meadows. They fish in their ponds, learn to handle firearms and shoot deer, rabbits and turkeys. They work as a family in the garden, raising, harvesting and canning their own vegetables.

Farm kids learn to keep good records on their livestock. When they raise and sell a 4-H calf, they can calculate the profit gained after deducting feed, vet medicines and other costs. They typically know how to stand on their own two feet and give project talks, or give oral reasons for judging a class of lambs or swine. Many of them earn leadership roles in church, 4-H or FFA, so they can moderate a meeting to perfection using Robert's Rules of Order. They learn early in life the tactics of conservation—how to keep topsoil from washing into Oklahoma; how to plant wind barriers and how to recognize grass-cheating weeds that need to be sprayed. Any farm kid can handle a paint brush, spade a garden, pull worms from tomato plants, gather hen eggs, mow grass, groom animals and take one grain of wheat, bite down on it and determine if it's time to start the combine.

And, this girl thinks her resume might be lackluster?

Oh, I don't think so.

Put her to work in a hardware store, newspaper office or grocery store, and she will enter the front door looking for things to do. It's that way with kids who grow up as farm and ranch kids. Their resume is written on their foreheads and in their hearts. They should never apologize. Never.

We know the farm provides incredible contribution opportunities. More importantly, work connects us to our humanity and to God. As we move away from a central theology of Genesis 3, let's dig into what it means to have a Genesis 1 theology. A theology that starts a long time ago on a farm, the first farm. A Genesis chapter 1 theology looks more like this…

God created the world and called it good. Then, He created man in His image and told man to bear this image in the world. He placed a man in the garden (a very farm-like place) and told him to work it and take care of it. Unfortunately, Adam disobeyed God, and because of this, sin has entered the world. We now live in a fallen and broken world which has separated us from God. Fortunately, Jesus came to earth to show us what it looks like to bear His image in this broken and fallen world; He showed us how to treat people and be a light within the darkness. We are thankful that Jesus died to save us, and we will have eternal life through participation in His death, burial, and resurrection.

A Genesis 1 theology seems to be more complete and has a different centrality. While Genesis 3 theology focuses on our brokenness, this Genesis 1 theology focuses on our image-bearing nature. In other words, this theology centers itself on man bearing God's image in the world. God created man, put man on a farm, and said, "Work it. Take care of it."

I grew up in the church as a preacher's kid, graduated from a Christian high school, and have an undergraduate degree in Bible. Still, with all of that, I for some reason always thought work came after the fall. I started to look back through different children's ministry resources, and it all made sense as to why I felt this way. I saw pictures like this:

First, man was put in the garden.

Then, the man messed up.

RAISING CONTRIBUTORS
IN A CULTURE OF CONSUMERISM AND SKEPTICISM

Then, the man toiled at work.

This was my felt board theology of the account of the fall. It wasn't until recently that I realized the significance of the fact that work came before the fall. Built into our God-given humanity is the call to work and contribute. Work is a part of our image-bearing nature. It is good; it is very good.

When your theology stems from Genesis chapter 1, a driving parental value is empowerment over protection

God made our kids in His image. So in other words, we are all made in the image of the ultimate Creator and contributor. Built into our humanity is this desire for purpose and meaning. While we may feel the cultural pressures to consume, God made each of us to contribute. While we may think consumption is the key to happiness, we find out that contribution is the ultimate key to happiness. Meaningful work that actually serves and benefits a neighbor thereby making a real difference in the world contributes to long-term happiness and well-being.

I was asked to speak at the chapel of a Christian university, which can sometimes be the worst speaking gig because you have a group of college kids in an auditorium that would rather be anywhere else, but I still agreed to do it. As I walked up to the podium, I looked out among a crowd of close to two thousand students. I told them that I had two statements, and I wanted them to stand if they found themselves fitting into one of the categories. First, I said please stand if while you were a high school student, you felt empowered by your church to bear the image of God in the world in which you lived. As I looked out, I was pleased to see an auditorium of college students standing. In fact, almost every student stood up to that statement. I then told them they could sit down, and I said, please stand if when you were in high school, you helped solve a city or global problem. To my surprise, only three students stood up in the entire two thousand-seat auditorium. This moment in time signified to me that there is an extreme disconnect between understanding we are made in the image of God and actually playing a role in bearing that image in meaningful ways.

I looked at these students and said, "I'm sorry." My apology was filled with sincerity, but it was also filled with humility because we, as the older generations, should know better. I believe that church leaders all over our country should stand in front of their congregations and proclaim these same words, "We're sorry." We are sorry we have failed children by not empowering them to be the person God has called them to be. We are sorry that we have low expectations for them and their faith. We are sorry that we have not connected their God-given humanity to their development as a person. Now bearing God's image isn't only done through solving global, state, or city issues. However, why not? Why not allow kids to participate in hard things to make the world better? Why limit it to being nice on the playground or sharing your toys?

In 1950, Erik Erikson, a popular psychologist, created what we know as the eight life stages, otherwise known as psychosocial development. Interestingly, three of the eight life stages happen at five years old or before. The two most important for this conversation are found in the life stages between five to twelve years old and twelve to eighteen years old.

Now, between ages twelve to eighteen, there is something really important going on in terms of the psychology of identity. Children are beginning to develop their identity, and there are two aspects of identity that are being developed; first, their sexual identity, and second, their occupational identity.

Now sexual identity is more complex than an average Christian parent wants to understand. No judgment, but in our parenting journey, how often do we discuss our child's sexual identity? We don't, and as a hypocrite myself, I don't plan to in this book. This is just something that as Christians and churches we do a poor job of. Unfortunately, culture does a terrific job of planting seeds of sexual identity. As Christian parents and churches, we must start making the conversation around being made in His image serious and intentional for the sake of our kids' sexual identity.

The second aspect of identity is called the occupational identity. Again, built into our humanity is this desire for purpose and meaning. While God made us in His image, He made us in the image of the ultimate Creator and contributor. We have a deep desire in our humanity to consume, but we are made to contribute. What is interesting about the occupational identity is that it connects back to the life stage of five to twelve. Erik Erikson says, "While all children need their hours and days of make-believe in games, they all, sooner or later, become dissatisfied and disgruntled without a sense of being useful, without a sense of being able to make things and make them well and even perfectly: this is what I call the sense of industry." This is why children love to build, create, and help. It's the reason why Fisher Price makes a killing on toys like vacuum cleaners, lawn mowers, kitchen sets, tool sets and the other activities where kids can mirror their parents doing real work. Kids want to be helpful and purposeful. It's just built into their DNA.

So we know that from a human development perspective, meaningfulness is a critical part of human development; we know that God Himself called us into a purpose-driven life. We all cognitively understand these things. So what's the problem? In a nationwide study of individuals from age twelve to twenty-six, only 20 percent were able to articulate their purpose in life and had found something meaningful enough in life to dedicate themselves to. We have stripped away meaningfulness, responsibility, and purpose in our children's lives and have filled it with games, technology, and media. We have stunted human development. From the earliest of scripture to the best of psychology, we know that we are made to contribute yet we continue to lower the contribution expectations for our children.

Practical tip. Set high expectations. The dissonance between our current expectations for kids and those just generations ago poses new and interesting questions as it relates to spirituality. Traditionally, as parents, we set the bar for academics high; maybe we push our children in an extracurricular pursuit, but what about our expectations to contribute? I am reminded of the movie *Stand and Deliver*. A group of high school teachers are in a meeting with the school administration, and they are discussing low test scores and poor academic performance. The teachers begin down a trail of negativity while one of the teachers announces that he is leaving the school.

However, one teacher sits there quietly at the end of the table. The principal says, "I am sure there is not a teacher in this room that isn't doing everything they possibly can for our students."

Mr. Escalante raises his hand. "I'm not." He went on to say, "Students will rise to the level of expectations we give them."

When I created a culture of contribution in the school I led, I again and again watched students rise to the occasion in the way they loved each other, searched after community needs, and sought after solutions. Our children are capable of changing their schools, their churches, their communities, and may I boldly say, our world.

When your theology stems from Genesis chapter 1, a driving parental value is development over happiness

Dr. Christian Smith said:

> Our teens are wasting some of the best years of their lives and never reaching their full God-

given potential. They never attempt things that stretch, grow, and strengthen them. They end up weak and unprepared for the amazing future that could have been. They like the low expectations and freedom, but they are really being robbed.

Our culture is seeking to take the hearts of our children captive through the narrative of consumption. Our desire should be to form their hearts in such an engaging way that they pursue contributing to society, families, churches, schools, and friends through the gospel narrative.

Besides protection, one of the significant adversaries to contribution is one's comfort level. Currently, we have a generation of teenagers that are very comfortable in their faith walk. My friend Ken Parker is the cofounder and CEO of NextThought, a company focused on connecting learners everywhere, building engaging communities, and creating collaborative content. In 2016, Ken gave the commencement address to the graduates of Oklahoma Christian University. He titled his address Don't Get Comfortable.

Ken focused on three points with the graduates:

- Comfort is almost always bad.
- To reach your furthest potential, you must be uncomfortable.
- Get started! It is never too late.

Comfortable. We tend to look at this word very positively in our culture. In fact, until recently I am not sure a negative thought ever crossed my mind when I heard this word. Comfortable. When I hear it, I think of my bed, my recliner, chicken fried steak, ice cream… you get the point.

When it comes to growing, however, being comfortable doesn't get me there. In fact, the only thing that grows when you're comfortable is your waistband. Comfortable does not help me become more mature, more knowledgeable, healthier, or more Christlike. Again, you get the point.

This leads me to a graduation ceremony on Friday, May 20, 2016. I was sitting on stage about to hand our seniors their diplomas (a great group I may add). I have Ken Parker's commencement address in the back of my mind, and one of our valedictorians, William Lin, gets to the podium to give his speech. I sat awed at his wisdom. With his permission, here is the transcript of that speech:

> *Do you remember those times when you got a little tired and then took a break? When you fell asleep comfortably and on time?*
>
> *Or do you remember when you continued work long after you were exhausted? When you stayed up all night studying?*
>
> *Most of my memories don't come from doing what I wanted to do. Even my fondest memories don't come from my wants. The things I cherish the most now are the things I disliked back then. I never wanted to participate in all of Mrs. Campbell's academic events. I never wanted to join an orchestra. I never wanted to get a job teaching children how to swim. But now I look back and see that those are the best parts of life. I never even wanted to give a valedictorian speech... Well actually I still don't. So, obviously, there have been some instances where I haven't grown to love something that I hate, but that's all part of the experience. You do what you hate to find out what you love.*
>
> *Now class, good job on making it this far, but from here, we still only have as much chance as anyone else. We're not prestigious. We're not the number one seed. We ARE different, but then again, everyone else is told the same thing. Don't kid yourself by seeking only what you love and thinking you'll be happy. There will always be disappointments, so instead of avoiding them, indulge in them, because*

> *it's the difficulties and unexpected that's memorable. What truly defines you.*
>
> *So I'd like to thank those who forced me to do what I hated, who kept my life imperfect. You know who you are and I don't want to read off a list of people, so...yeah.*
>
> *So just let me leave you with one piece of advice: Don't just do what you love. You'll find the experience to be much better.*

I couldn't articulate that message better myself! If we want children to live out the gospel, we must foster passion not mediocrity, creativity not practicalities, boldness not passivity, risk-taking not risk aversion, consciousness not selfishness, and contribution not consumption.

Practical tip. We should allow our children to fail. For children to be able to deal with life's difficulties and obstacles, they must practice dealing with these difficulties and obstacles in a safe environment. Tim Elmore, founder of Growing Leaders, suggested parents make three major mistakes:

- Risk too little
- Rescue too quickly
- Reward too frequently

It is crucial that we allow our students to fail, struggle, and suffer in safe environments and at developmentally appropriate times. Often, life's events are uncontrollable, but when we can allow students to deal with adversity, we must not miss the opportunity. This is why my plagiarism misstep or my all-star travesty were perfect developmental moments for me.

When your theology stems from Genesis chapter 1, a driving parental value is accountability over advocacy

When I have the opportunity to visit with parents, I start with a simple question: what five character traits do you want to see in your child when they turn thirty years old? Typically, parents come up with some really good answers to this question but rarely do their parental actions, values, or practices align with forming these traits into their children. As we go back to the story about the family upset about their child's softball statistics, arguably, you can believe that softball taught their daughter character traits like teamwork, responsibility, hard work, punctuality, and the like. The problem lies in the obsession that overtakes a family within the context of the activity. Quickly, a good activity meant to teach good things becomes an obsession, steering our children from anything important we ultimately want for them. To me, the best words of wisdom for my parenting came from a quote of C. S. Lewis from one of his sermons. In paraphrase form he said, *"You can only get first things first by putting second things second."* This seems simple.

As I see it, we have first things in life and second things in life. Second things are not bad things; they are just second. Second things may be academics, athletic achievement, or even fine art activities. First things, to name a few, would be faith, character, and family. As parents, we can easily get confused by these two things because we believe second things produce first things. For example, we will say that because my son plays football (second thing), he will develop responsibility (first thing). However, I don't buy this premise. I do believe that second things can play a role in forming first things.

However, second things can quickly confuse our children and move them away from first things. An organization called 3D Coaching has done significant research on how to use sports for intentionally shaping children:

> The jury is out, and the verdict is in! Reliable research has conclusively shown us that sport, left to itself, erodes moral character in the

RAISING CONTRIBUTORS
IN A CULTURE OF CONSUMERISM AND SKEPTICISM

lives of competitive athletes. However, other evidence has surfaced to show us that sport presents an incredibly powerful opportunity to pass on meaningful life lessons to athletes, if a coach is deliberate about teaching and modeling moral character.

As parents, we often put second things in front of first things, and before we know it, our time, schedule, and entire life are centered around second things. We justify it because we think our kids love it; we feed the obsession, and we lose grasp on reality. Second things can teach and foster first things, but it must be done intentionally and purposefully. Otherwise, our hopes for raising *first-thing* people fail.

As someone that has witnessed time and time again children drifting away into the abyss of burnout and depression, I plead with you to press pause on the madness of second things. At least for a moment, step back, and reflect on your life, your priorities, your children, and your family. We end up allowing our kids to spend so much time on second things that we unintentionally develop *second-thing* people. Our kids leave high school as a baseball player and quickly graduate to find themselves going through an identity crisis because they aren't a baseball player anymore. Or they are the valedictorian and they view themselves as the smart kid, but now they are in college and aren't the smartest anymore. Who are they? They are second-thing people.

Practical tip. List out five character traits you want to see in your child when they turn thirty years old. Then on a second page, write out what you have done in the past six weeks to intentionally foster those five things. If you feel like you need to do better, create a six-week plan to foster those traits in your child.

CHAPTER 5

Called to Contribute

> We all have different gifts, so we all have different ways of saying to the world who we are.
>
> —Mr. Rogers

I love this quote by Johann Wolfgang von Goethe, "There are two things children should get from their parents: roots and wings." Over the years I have attempted to create a cultural framework in our parents, churches, and schools that allow our students to learn from failure and responsibility. As parents, do we advocate so much for our kids that we lose sight of the value of accountability? What are we even advocating for? Fairness? Do we believe our child's world should be fair?

Technology is not going away, and the honest truth is that our children will continue to be on their technology for hours a day. In fact, as I am writing this section, I am witnessing my Generation Alpha daughter stand in front of our fifty-inch television, holding the Apple TV remote, and talking into it saying, "Open Netflix."

The expectations our American culture has for teens is another aspect that won't change during this generation. The tension of wanting to protect our kids will never leave us, and our desire to have happy kids will continue to create tensions between their happiness and their development. The question this book longs to answer is,

RAISING CONTRIBUTORS
IN A CULTURE OF CONSUMERISM AND SKEPTICISM

what can we do? What are the practicalities that can help us develop faithfulness in our children?

Often, in discussing faith development with children, we can spend time on theology, sociology, and philosophy, but we miss the practicalities on what all this means and what we can be doing. Dr. James K.A. Smith argued in his book, *You Are What You Love*, that culture is forming us in powerful ways, and in many ways we are blind to it. So how do we create a culture of faith development while our children are heavily engaged in cultural pursuits? Even our children who are open to dialogue about faith, are connected to a church family, and believe in the gospel story are at risk of being overtaken by the engaging culture of our world. Years ago, Dr. Larry Taylor, author of *Running with the Horses*, said something at a conference that still haunts me as a parent today: "If I were Satan and I knew I could not take your faith from you I would do everything in my power to keep you from handing it down to your children." That statement is a demand for intentionality in working with our kids.

It is important to understand that one of the most important things we can do to reach our children is to create cultures that foster formation. Faith development is not a by-product of being good and nice to children. As we look at our culture at large, running away and hiding is not an option. Well, it's not a good option at least. We have seen people try this strategy throughout time, and in fact, there are sects of individuals that value this strategy. I am not one.

I am reminded of the M. Night Shyamalan's movie called *The Village* that came out in 2004. The movie is set in an Amish-like community away from civilization and hidden in the woods. The viewer is made to believe that this was filmed in an earlier era before technology and the conveniences of the new age. Spoiler alert: it was all a facade. We come to find out that this family has been living in a community in the woods that started in the 1970s. They began the community because of the trauma they had experienced in their normal lives, and they believed if they could simplify and strip culture away, they could live happy, safe, and meaningful lives only to find out that they couldn't escape the snake in the garden. So if we can't escape culture, how do we interact with it?

In his book *Culture Making*, Andy Crouch explains that as Christians, we have three ways to interact with or view culture:

1. We can critique culture.
2. We can condemn culture.
3. We can create culture.

Now allow me to share some aspects of the culture I want to create for my kids. Here are four principles for creating a culture that can cultivate contribution in our children:

1. A culture that points children to their ultimate contributor, God
2. A culture that utilizes every aspect of community to cultivate contributors
3. A culture that helps children identify their gifts and guides them to contribute their gifts to the world
4. A culture that acknowledges that *cultivating* is an intentional act

These four concepts are active and encompass both the cognitive aspect of faith and the image-bearing aspect of faith. On top of this, our cultures must promote action in both our children and the adults in their lives. So we must understand that a contributor culture is an active culture that does these things:

1. Engages children
2. Sees value in learning from mistakes
3. Promotes creating
4. Promotes service-oriented learning opportunities

It is my desire that through a culture like the one highlighted above, our children learn several important things. First, children learn to know that God is the ultimate contributor and redeemer of all things. Second, they learn to know that everything was created for His purpose. Third, I want them to know that humankind was created in God's image to contribute toward His purpose as His craftsmen. It is my hope that we will see this knowledge in our children through their actions. Lastly, let's not only hold them to higher standards, but let's put a support network in place that empowers and equips them to do amazing things. Our American culture says they need to wait until they are older, but a contributor culture is saying, "Do it now!"

- We need cultures that empower them to do bold things with their faith.
- We need cultures that empower them to be true image bearers of Christ.
- We need cultures that empower them to do great things for their communities and their world.

Many of the protections for kids have been good, but we threw the baby out with the bathwater when our culture adopted its current view of adolescence. My concern as of late is that this has seeped into our churches, schools, and families. As a whole, we have not created a culture of empowerment among the emerging generations. Statistically, we missed the boat with the millennial generation, but it's not too late for Generations Alpha and Z. We can make some changes, but we need to be swift.

In a book titled *Called to Create*, Joran Rayner quotes preacher John Piper, "God made humans in His image so that the world would be filled with reflectors of God. Images of God. Seven billion statues of God. So nobody would miss the point of creation." Scripture clearly tells us that all children are created in the image of God, and all children are created to contribute to the world as His workmanship. It is our humanity that begs each of us to be image bearers in the world. Dr. Martin Luther King Jr. said it my favorite way, "Human progress never rolls in on wheels of inevitability; it comes through the tireless efforts of men willing to be coworkers with God." I believe a powerful question we must be asking ourselves as we reflect on the cultures we create is this: Do we have a culture that equips and empowers children to bear His image in the world?

Are we building and empowering coworkers with God? As parents, we must be asking ourselves, *Have I created an environment within my family that encourages my children to reflect His image in meaningful and powerful ways?*

Practical tip. Truth check! Examine your current family culture, and be honest with yourself. Do you really have a culture that allows a fifteen-year-old to truly be a coworker for God? To capture this emerging generation, we must begin taking an active role in their empowerment. Culture is creating consumers. We should be cultivating contributors.

Now that we know what a culture of contribution looks like, let's turn our attention to the types of strategies I think are best for formation. I would argue that we can only cultivate contributors through an intentional framework of creating experiences because it is the most powerful formation strategy we have as Christians.

Create memories for children

I vividly remember a time in fifth grade when I did not bring my current event assignment to school. On Fridays we were to cut out a newspaper story and present it to our class. I got to class and had that *uh-oh moment*—I forgot! Luckily, my buddy, the overachiever, brought two newspaper articles to school that day. He was kind enough to share one with me. It worked perfectly, and I got an A on the assignment. However, there was an issue. My mom knew that it was a current event day, and she knew I didn't cut out an article. So when I got home my mom asked, "So how did your current event go?"

I didn't think about how all-knowing she was, so I responded, "Great, I got a 100!"

To her surprise she said, "How did this happen? I know you didn't do it."

I told her that I had used my buddy's article, and it worked out great. What came next was the memory-making part of this story that sticks with me as an adult. She said, "On Monday you will pull Mrs. Smith aside and you will tell her that you did not bring that article on your own, that you did not do your homework, and that you are sorry for deceiving her."

I spent the rest of that weekend sick to my stomach about the conversation I would have to have with Mrs. Smith. Monday rolled around, and I asked Mrs. Smith if we could talk in the hallway. I cried my way through a pathetic apology, but I did it. I apologized to an adult and acknowledged that I tried to deceive her. I learned an invaluable lesson that day that has formed a standard in my adult life.

It's memories like this that can stick with us and may even drive our actions today. It's pretty amazing that something that happened so long ago can cultivate current thoughts, beliefs, and values for how we interact in our world. Memories shape the soundtracks of our lives.

As a child, I had the opportunity to grow up as a preacher's kid. This childhood provided me the opportunity to have some meaningful faith experiences from a very early age. At the age of three, I would lead singing at our church in large corporate worship. My father even built a small podium that my children use today. I remember using this podium all throughout my earliest years of life. Sometimes I would use it as I preached to a number of stuffed animals lined up on the floor against my bedroom wall, and other times, I would use it as I led our family devotional in the evenings. The experiences surrounding that podium shaped who I am today.

All through the Bible, we see examples of the power of experience. In the Old Testament, Israel's national identity originated in their exodus from Egypt. This event was so important that God instructed them to annually observe the Passover ceremony because He realized that a time would come when a generation would no longer remember the exodus without a memory aid. The Passover ceremony was important because it was a reminder of God's faithfulness. Practically, this created a great object lesson for parents to retell the story of God's faithfulness for generations. Wrapped up in Passover is a memory that has the power to give hope.

What's also interesting about experience is that sometimes we are moved by the experiences of others. Our generation never experienced firsthand fighting in World War II, and yet we have a deep appreciation and honor for those that served in that world-changing war.

I believe as educators, parents, and ministers, we are in the business of creating memories through experience. In the conscious and unconscious, intentional and unintentional, we are creating memories in our children that will last a lifetime. I pray that as loving Christian adults, we use everyday circumstances to create memories that lead our children to God and His kingdom.

One of my nightly dad duties when my kids were younger was bath and bedtime. I enjoy this time. It allowed me to turn the busyness of life off and pay full attention to my kids each night. Before bed, we did the same routine of reading stories and singing a song. When my son was around two, he always wanted to sing "Jesus Loves Me", or as he called it, Jesus Bible. The books he was most interested in during this time were those related to the alphabet. You remember what these books were like; every page had a letter on it and that letter was connected to a word. A is for apples. It was pretty amazing to see his knowledge grow in regard to identifying letters and making their corresponding sound.

At some point, he will learn to take this basic knowledge and will begin reading these books to me. We must acknowledge that reading could be the most important, fundamental skill our children learn in their early education. Once a child learns to read, their capacity for learning is almost limitless. They can teach themselves almost anything they want to learn. Because of this, I'm convinced that the most important thing we do in education is to teach students to read. In many ways, literacy is the beginning of all knowledge. I will take this a step further and argue that as Christians, we teach our children to read something far greater than words. We teach our children to read culture and faith.

Being intentional about this is more important now than ever, and here is why. Speed, accumulation, instant gratification, and technology are just a few words that sum up the American culture in which our children are being raised. None of these things are inherently bad, but we must remember that it's our job not to let the hearts of our children be taken by the things of this world. Country music group Lady Antebellum sings a song called "Compass" which highlights an interesting perspective of our culture:

> So let your heart sweetheart be your compass when you're lost
> And you should follow it wherever it may go.
> When it's all said and done you can walk instead of run
> 'Cause no matter what you'll never be alone

The most significant deception our culture tells our children is to let their hearts be their compass for life. Whether we want to admit it or not, at a foundational level, we are all driven by our emotions, feelings, and desires. This is why many of us continue to do things we know we shouldn't do. I know I should never eat the Chicka-Chicka Boom-Boom from Chuy's Tex-Mex because I know it is bad for me, but I love it too much. We all have these things we know we ought not to do but we do them anyway. At a basic level this is okay, but if not kept in check, it can create devastating consequences.

We all understand two important truths. First, we know our emotions, feelings, and desires play a pivotal role in our actions. Secondly, we know we live in a culture that encourages our children to be led by their hearts. So instead of resisting this, let's use this to our advantage in helping our children read culture and faith. Let's provide our children with experiences that continue to mold who they are. This is why I value experience in the lives of our children. Our experiences form internal desires and create a piggy bank of memories that we draw upon when making current decisions. Through the experiences of life, we can help form their hearts and shape the actions of tomorrow.

Bearing God's image

As we start in Genesis, we see God as the ultimate contributor. He created the world we inhabit and the bodies we utilize. He created man, put him in the garden, and told man to work it and take care of it. Since the beginning, God called man to contribute. So we have a contribution calling—a calling to contribute to God's creation in meaningful ways, a calling to bring people into relationship with him, and a calling to be difference makers. A calling to contribute to the workplace, academia, family, church, and connecting God to each of these aspects in our lives.

Through scripture, we see man's contribution to our world and to God's plan for our world. Interestingly, some of the most impactful contributors in scripture are not adults as we would define them today; rather, they were teenagers. We see David as a young shepherd becoming a giant slayer and a man after God's own heart. We see God call Jeremiah to be a prophet, and he even pleaded to God, "I am too young!" Yet Jeremiah went on to be a great mouthpiece for God. We see Esther, whose courage helped to save a nation, which demonstrated that God can use anyone to fulfill His purpose and change the world.

How about Daniel and his three friends? They are in their teenage years when they stood up and committed not to defile themselves with royal food and drink. Did you know Samuel was about eleven years old when he first heard God's call? Let's not forget about the young girl who pointed Naaman to Elisha for healing and the apostle Paul's young nephew who warned him about a plot on his life. There was the little boy who responded to the Savior by contributing his lunch to help Jesus feed the masses. Of course there is Mary the mother of Jesus, the very picture of humility and devotion.

The Bible is full of youth doing amazing things for their faith. One of my favorite quotes of all time comes from Rob Bell's *Velvet Elvis* as he discussed the disciples, "Jesus took a group of boys and changed the course of human history."

While over time humanity has contributed in great ways from a young age, it is clear that from the beginning, we have deviated from the plan, and in many ways, we are contributing to the brokenness we now see in the world. Consumption is the new norm for teens in our culture. Entire industries have taken off like music, movies, fashion, and fast food. So here we sit today, and we ask the question,

RAISING CONTRIBUTORS
IN A CULTURE OF CONSUMERISM AND SKEPTICISM

how do we reclaim contribution for our emerging generation? How do we cultivate contributors? The answer lies somewhere within the framework of spiritual formation. Dr. James K.A. Smith tells us, "The Biblical doctrine of creation is not just about where we came from; it is about where we are. It's not just about who we are, but whose we are. It's not just a statement from our past; it's a calling to our future." So let's look at some of these future contributors.

When visiting a school in Houston, Texas, I came across a young man named Emmanuel. Emmanuel was a student at Westbury Christian School (WCS) located in Houston, Texas. Emmanuel brought a program to WCS called Health Occupations Students of America (HOSA), an international student organization recognized by the US Department of Education for its twofold mission—to expose students to the health-care field through information, competition, and service while promoting and supporting career opportunities in the industry. It was important to Emmanuel that this organization be entirely student led, and Westbury Christian School has given Emmanuel an office on campus. Over time, all administrative and leadership roles transferred from the adult advisors to the student officers. A major goal of Emmanuel's was not only to help the community through HOSA but empower students to be contributors in any capacity they were given. Since its inception, Emmanuel has grown the membership by 500 percent.

He introduced quarterly speaking events, and over the course of a couple of years, had created partnerships with Texas Children's Hospital, UT College of Dentistry, UH College of Pharmacy, Miracle-Ear, MD Anderson Cancer Center Blood Bank, Smith Ledesma Law, Thurgood Marshall School of Law, Bee Busy Wellness Center, US Marines, Houston Fire Department, Houston Forensic Science Center, and Who We Play For sponsored by the Cody Stephens Foundation.

In connection with the MD Anderson Cancer Center, he created the Spring into Good Health Fair where one hundred people in the Houston area received free medical services and the following year increased the services to where a total of three hundred members of the community received free medical care. Emmanuel, with his executive team, decided to expand the health fair to include career services in order to pique the interests of more children and students. The fair was named the Create Your Future Health and Career Fair. The city mayor and a Texas congressman agreed to attend the event. The WCS HOSA chapter received a certificate of special congressional recognition on behalf of the local congressman. Due to the immense success of WCS's work, their school was selected by the Texas HOSA State Association to host a Spring Leadership Conference, which brought around two thousand students to the WCS campus to participate in competitive events and lectures to better equip them to be contributors to society in a meaningful and impactful way.

Another amazing young contributor is named Holden Hill. He considers himself to be an American-born lover of Jesus Christ, adventurer, author, and aspiring motivational speaker. Holden is the son of two entrepreneurial parents and is the oldest of five siblings. At sixteen years old, Holden Hill set out on a high school-long journey to interview five hundred Christ-following leaders from across the United States and the world. Some of these leaders include Bob Goff, Lecrae, Dave Ramsey, Craig Groeschel, John Maxwell, and Christine Caine. Through that journey, God used Holden's personal struggles and battles to erupt an untamable fire in his heart for Jesus—a fire that he now sees as his calling to spread the gospel across the world. Holden used these five hundred interviews to write a book that was published in 2018 called *Bring the Fire*.

Growing up in a passionate, outspoken family, Holden discovered his passion for writing and speaking at an early age. With a love for telling stories and eliciting emotion, he often uses his talents on stage as a way to challenge people with the same questions he wrestles with himself. Questions about life, purpose, and God. And he sees speaking as a way to help others find the truth behind those questions—his motivation behind it all.

Another group of amazing contributors are a group of young ladies from Tennessee and were students at Friendship Christian School. Their names are Anna Kate Armstrong, Pryce Jordan Daniels, Jessica Cherry, and Scottie Smit. These girls developed the

RAISING CONTRIBUTORS
IN A CULTURE OF CONSUMERISM AND SKEPTICISM

84 Days ministry. Eighty-four days is the number of days a young girl will miss school if she doesn't have proper feminine hygiene. These girls developed a ministry designed to empower women by providing reusable pads/menstrual cups, feminine hygiene training, self-defense, and the message of Jesus empowering women. The girls have performed the ministry in five villages in Nicaragua, impacting seven hundred women, and eleven villages in Uganda/Kenya, impacting twelve hundred women in the last year. Not only have these girls traveled the world, but they have raised their own funds by speaking to many church and civic groups about 84 Days.

Finally, I would like to introduce you to a group of young ladies at Oklahoma Christian Academy, Meg Garner, Brooke Landes, and Amanda Fike. These young ladies had a vision for helping others, both at their school and in the community. They created a fundraising week at school called Do Unto Others Week, otherwise known as DUO week. As self-admitted introverts, these ladies challenged themselves to move outside of their comfort zones in order to be image bearers of Christ. It was an honor to be able to watch each of them grow and become more confident in leading others. Their humility, drive, and passion demonstrated what it truly means to be a contributor. They decided that they wanted to help foster children in the state of Oklahoma. These young ladies set out on a mission with a goal of raising $15,000.

I remember having conversations with some of the adults in these young ladies' lives because they were worried they wouldn't make their goal of $15,000. The concern was that if they do not hit their goal, they would be devastated and feel like failures. As you know, my response was so what! If they raise $5,000, that is more than $0, and if they fail, this is the best time of their lives to do that. These young ladies surpassed their goal and to my amazement raised $50,000 for foster kids in our state. It is amazing what can happen when you create a culture that empowers children to bear God's image.

We must begin pushing, examining, evaluating, and questioning spiritual formation strategies of the old and seeking engaging strategies for today. We must begin asking questions like

1. how do we empower our children and families to engage in the gospel narrative
2. how do we help children see their role in the bigger story God is telling?
3. how can we help children recognize their potential inside themselves?
4. what does it look like for our family to follow Jesus?
5. what role does our church have in restoring and redeeming the brokenness in our community?
6. how do we help students connect academic content to the ultimate contributor?
7. how do we challenge our children to look beyond themselves and impact others while they live in a world consumed with self?
8. how do we connect real-life experiences to the ultimate contributor?
9. how do we create habitual patterns of spiritual disciplines in three-year-olds, kindergarteners, first graders, and the like?
10. how do we get children to see that in a life of contributing, they will find freedom?
11. how do we take our youth group from knowing about Christ to contributing for Christ?

From a church perspective, more specific questions could be asked:

1. How many teens are contributing to corporate worship at our church?
2. How are we connecting the God-given gifts of your teens to contribute to the larger church community?

3. Are our youth group contributors to our church or consumers of it?

These questions all connect us back to a dialogue of how we ought to cultivate or form the hearts of our children.

Let us now create cultures that dare greatly to engage and form this emerging generation. Let us attempt to try new strategies and know they might fail, but it is in failing that you learn, it is in failing that you grow, and it is in failing that you challenge kids to reach new heights for the gospel of Jesus Christ. Be authentic in your strategies. Be genuine in your relationships, humble in your efforts, and bold in your actions. I hope to create a movement of cultivating contributors, and I invite you into the conversation.

PART 2

Raising Contributors in a Culture of Skepticism

PART 2

Introduction

Part 2 of this book focuses on the faith climate in which our kids are living. We will dig deep into what is happening at a faith level and take a look at the entertainment that they are consuming on a daily basis. They are being formed every day by the culture they inhabit. As readers, let's go back into our own childhoods and remember the wonderful childhood stories of Mary Poppins, Aladdin, and so many other narratives that shaped our upbringings. How did those stories shape us, and what are the new generation of stories shaping our children?

    I will argue that the entertainment we consume even at an early age play a significant role in how we approach faith and even the Holy Scriptures. While we must empower our kids to contribute and live out God's calling, we also must help guide our children to believe in God eternal. We cannot fully contribute His image without first believing in the God that made us. Since the 90s, we have been seeing research leading us to believe our kids are falling away from their faith. George Barna in the 90s almost predicted what we are seeing today almost like a fortune teller. Why is this the case? What is happening in our culture that could lead to some of this? Let's explore.

CHAPTER 6

Meaning and Truth

Are you able to believe in a loving presence who desires the best for you and the whole universe? With all the sadness and destruction, negativity and rage expressed throughout the world, it's tough not to wonder where the loving presence is. Well, we don't have to look very far. Deep within each of us is a spark of the divine just waiting to be used to light up a dark place. The only thing is—we have the free choice of using it or not. That's part of the mysterious truth of who we human beings are.

—Mr. Rogers

For the rest of this book, let me be your tour guide as I discuss the generational tensions of understanding and using Scripture. We look back through time in an attempt to understand our present and explore the world of transcendence as we know it. For years now, I have felt tensions between the ways younger and older generations approach Scripture. This is best illustrated through the story of Jennifer. She sat toward the front of her tenth-grade English class at a Christian school. She was one of the top performing students in her grade and sat there intently as the teacher began to lecture.

The teacher began to discuss the miracle story of Jesus feeding the five thousand. To the teacher, this was a matter-of-fact reference during a lecture in her English class. Little did she know Jennifer would make a comment that still impacts her today. As Mrs. Johnson was discussing this well-known story of Jesus, a gentle voice interrupted her mid-sentence. Jennifer, a polite student and not one to typically interrupt a teacher during a lecture, caught Mrs. Johnson off guard. Furthermore, the interruption was followed with a plea for the teacher to stop talking.

"Mrs. Johnson, can we not talk about this? I don't see any way this story can be true, and if it's not true, it destroys my entire faith. Like, how did the baskets show up? How did all the food appear? How could all the people even hear Jesus without a microphone?"

Her concerns about the text were specific in nature. They also were surrounded with *how statements*. How did the food appear? How did the baskets appear? How could they hear Jesus talking? Mrs. Johnson sat stunned as Jennifer looked at her and asked her not to talk about the feeding of the five thousand. This was a young student that Mrs. Johnson went to church with; she had good Christian parents, she was even raised going to Sunday school. At that moment, it was the nature of Mrs. Johnson to immediately begin defending the authority of the text, which arguably would be the nature of most adults in that situation. Feeling the need to defend the text to Jennifer is one of the greatest generational tensions I am noticing. This tension has haunted me over recent years because it makes me wonder, did the authority of the story need to be defended at that moment? Maybe so, but it isn't the best starting place in a critical conversation over Scripture with a Gen Zer.

Jennifer's experience is not found in isolation. A minister friend of mine Travis Akins was telling me about his experience teaching Revelation to eleventh-grade students. He was in Revelation chapter 4:

> After this I looked, and there before me was a door standing open in heaven. And the voice I had first heard speaking to me like a trumpet said, 'Come up here, and I will show you what must take place after this.' At once I was in the Spirit,

and there before me was a throne in heaven with someone sitting on it.

Travis said the students quickly began asking questions like, "How did the door get there?" or "Where did the door even come from?" The students wanted the backstory to the story itself. They needed to be able to rationally explain the story, and without rationalization, the story couldn't be believed.

Why are these children asking these very practical questions about our text? Why are they struggling to lean into the transcendent nature of the Scriptures? Why can't they trust the inspiration of the Bible and appreciate the beauty of its intent? I want to spend the rest of the book unpacking these questions.

If you recall, I use the birth year of 1995 for Generation Z. This is because there was an underground cultural liturgy powered by a powerful visual storytelling machine that gained power in 1986 and exploded publicly in 1995, which arguably is a driving factor of some of the faith issues we are now seeing. On November 22, 1995, Pixar's *Toy Story* hit theaters and was the highest grossing film on its opening weekend, earning over $373 million worldwide. In 1986, a new animation group named Pixar was formally created, and I believe Pixar has impacted more than the screens we watch. A year after the release of *Toy Story*, Disney and Pixar announced that they would jointly produce five movies over the next ten years. These movies were *A Bug's Life* (1998), *Toy Story 2* (1999), *Monsters Inc.* (2001), *Finding Nemo* (2003), and *Cars* (2006). Since the birth of Generation Alpha, Pixar has produced seventeen more hits.

Regardless of the details of generational birthdays, it's safe to say that Pixar significantly impacted millennials, Generation Z, and now Generation Alpha. If we are calling the millennial generation the iY generation, I am suggesting that Generation Z is the Pixar generation. They grew up in a world where Pixar beautifully created worlds where the make believe became a normal part of their lives. Now, Generation Alpha doesn't know anything else but the Pixar culture of storytelling. Over time, these beautifully developed fictional stories depicted seemingly real-life characters in amazing ways.

Arguably, this has produced a special Pixar reading of Scripture for our children. I describe this as the Pixar mindset being developed in our kids. It impacts the way they think, dream, and imagine stories in their own heads. It even impacts their big imaginations.

An interesting concept of Pixar and a very distinctive difference between Pixar and Disney is the desire Pixar has to mimic physics within their movies. It is almost a Pixar mandate to mimic laws of gravity and motion within their animated films. You will note in Pixar movies how realistic hair on the characters seems and how their hair almost realistically blows in the wind the way our hair would. Or the way characters fall at almost the same exact rate a person would fall in real life. A good example of this contrast is the differences found between Disney's *Mary Poppins* and Pixar's animated movie *Up*. It is interesting to note that *Up* was produced when Generation Alpha was being born and *Mary Poppins* hit the big screen in 1964. Most millennials would have grown up with Mary Poppins being a staple in their VHS collection.

The opening scenes of *Mary Poppins* may be one of the most iconic scenes of any Disney movie. You remember this scene vividly. It is time for the Banks family to begin interviewing for a new nanny. The nannies are lined up at the door and all the way around the block. They are all dressed alike with big black hats and black dresses from head to toe. But then a major wind gust comes through the scene. Everything and every nanny is blown away while here comes Mary Poppins flying through the sky. She's holding an umbrella and is unphased by the winds. She lands at the front door to promptly begin her interview with Mr. Banks.

Compare this Disney story with the Pixar animated movie *Up*. In *Up*, there is the famous scene of the retirement home center coming to pick up Mr. Fredricksen from the home he has lived in for years. He hands the man his suitcase and asks to say one last goodbye to his house. As you look around his front yard, you see hundreds of used helium tanks. You watch him throw furniture out of his house to make it lighter, and then you see helium balloons floating up above his house as he floats away into the air using sheets as sails to fly him to another far away city.

RAISING CONTRIBUTORS IN A CULTURE OF CONSUMERISM AND SKEPTICISM

During the Disney movie, Mary Poppins was able to fly with an umbrella defying any known realities while Mr. Fredricksen could only fly with thousands of helium balloons tied together. Why is this interesting? Pixar, in many ways, is creating rules within our imaginations. While Mary Poppins flies through the air in no logical way, one could see some logic in a significant amount of helium balloons sailing into the sky. Therefore, even the *fairy tales* our kids watch through Pixar make some level of sense, at least as we know it.

Disney fairy tales rarely had logic connected to them, but Pixar fairy tales are logical and more realistic. So when our kids come to Scripture, they need it to make sense. You see, when dealing with the Disney fairy tales, you have to suspend your belief, but within the Pixar fairy-tale world, there is a magic component that operates within rules that make sense for us.

A significant problem lies within the fact that the Bible, God, and Jesus do not operate within any rules as we know them. Richard Beck, a psychology professor at Abilene Christian University, described on stage in front of hundreds of college freshmen a concept called negativity dominance. He explained that when the pure and polluted come together, the pollutant is always the stronger force and the pure is the weaker source. In a humorous way, he illustrated this with an apple and a college student. In one hand he held a clean red apple and in another hand he held a piece of dog poop. He asked the student if she would take a bite of the apple, and she said she would. He then rubbed the dog poop on the clean apple and asked again. This time her response was enthusiastically no! Then, he took the apple and rubbed it all over the dog poop. Afterward, he asked her if she would eat the dog poop. Of course, the student's answer was similar—no!

He then wanted her to acknowledge the reasoning behind her enthusiastic no answers. The poop made the apple bad, but the apple did not make the poop good. In psychology, this is considered negativity dominance. In my layman's terms, bad makes a good thing bad, but a good thing never makes a bad thing good. In this scenario, the power sat with the dog poop (the negative).

As we look through the stories on the pages of our Scripture, we see that the Pharisees watch Jesus (positive) touching an unclean woman (negative), and in their minds, that contaminated Jesus. However, in the gospels, we see the opposite happening. When the unclean woman (negative) comes into contact with Jesus (positive), she becomes clean. The sick woman is healed, the blind man sees, and the leper lives. Jesus and much of Scripture defies reality and logic as we know it.

By creating real-life rules within their animated fairy tales, Pixar is shaping new imaginations. So when our kids come to Scripture, they need it to make sense and find logic in the story. The issue we find in Scripture is that this ancient text does not feel constrained by our societal norms, laws, psychology, or logic. So this tension plays out in the minds of our children. This is why Jennifer in her English class began asking her teacher very practical questions about the miracle story. How did the bread break into so many pieces, where did the bread come from, and where did the baskets come from? This is why the boys in Bible class can't understand how that door got there. When dealing with these Pixar generations, we must understand how they come to Scripture, and we must examine it in connection to the way older generations tend to come to Scripture. Dr. Root argued, "We live in a time when magic is left to movies and goddesses to models with sex appeal."

Trying to teach the complexities of Scripture to children in a Pixar world will not become easier over time. How will we ever help our children come to appreciate and know the depths of this ancient text? As I ponder this question, let me take you back to my childhood. I remember it like it was yesterday; she sat there in a small wooden chair wearing a faded dress with a flower pattern of blue, green, and red from top to toe. Her hair was Barbara Bush white, but when the fluorescent lights hit her hair just the right way, it was as blue as a Smurf. She was a sweet lady who had dedicated her life to teaching kids every Sunday morning around a wooden semicircle table. I, five or six years old at the time, sat in my button-up shirt and clip-on tie ready to sing and hopefully walk away that morning with a craft. Not yet eager to learn but ready to play and have a good time.

RAISING CONTRIBUTORS
IN A CULTURE OF CONSUMERISM AND SKEPTICISM

Sometimes we would sing songs about Jesus like "Jesus Loves Me," and other times we would sing songs that had little connection to faith. She would sing to us asking if we had come to Bible class in a boat or plane, neither of which were remotely possible. I have vivid memories during these years of learning the creation story through the powerful teaching tool of the flannel board. Mrs. Collier sat in her chair and shared the simplistic true story of how God created the world.

We have spent a significant amount of time in Genesis, so let's look at the first chapter of Genesis again. It's here that our Scripture starts, and in most cases, it's where Sunday school training begins to teach children about the origins of this great narrative. You may remember that cute song that teaches us the depths of creation. I poke fun at this song by saying it teaches us the *great depths* of creation because in many cases, our pure attempts to teach Scripture to children creates deep consequences by simplifying the complexities of the story. Do you remember this song?

>Day One, Day One
>God made the light when there was none.
>Day One, Day One.
>God cre-at-ed ever-y-thing!
>
>Day Two, Day Two
>God made clouds and the skies so blue
>Day Two, Day Two
>God cre-at-ed ever-y-thing!
>
>Day Three, Day Three
>God made green grass and flow'rs and trees
>Day Three, Day Three
>God cre-at-ed ever-y-thing!
>
>Day Four, Day Four
>God made sun, moon and stars gal-ore
>Day Four, Day Four
>God cre-at-ed ever-y-thing!

Day Five, Day Five
God made birds fly and fish a-live
Day Five, Day Five
God cre-at-ed ever-y-thing!

Day Six, Day Six
God made an'mals and man that day
Day Six, Day Six
God cre-at-ed ever-y-thing!

Day Seven, Day Seven
God rest-ed up a-bove in heav'n
Day Seven, Day Seven
God was fin-ished ever-y-thing!

Fast forward several years, and I am sitting in an undergraduate Bible class as a biblical text major at a prominent Christian university. Here my professor stood in front of the class not with blue hair but rather no hair at all. He wore a black suit, with a funeral-like tie, and a pudgy belly that always led to the front of his shirt being untucked. With fifty of my college-age peers sitting in a similar semicircle fashion but in bigger chairs and in an auditorium-style room, it was there I then learned the ever-complex narrative of the poetic creation account. Found in the dissonance between these two pure attempts of teaching me Scripture lies the heartbeat of what has haunted my theology, and through the years, have learned that I am not alone in this. My professor eloquently shared the other poetic creation accounts that were circulating at the time of the Genesis creation account. In fact, there were many groups of people attempting to explain the origin of the world. This explanation was all done through story.

These other creation accounts are not of particular interest to me in the discussion of faith formation, but what impacted me more was the understanding that the Bible sat within its own cultural narrative, and to truly understand the Bible, you needed to understand its culture. As a little boy, the creation story was literal, but now as a college kid, I am learning that it could be poetic. What is going on here? Was I lied to? This led me down a path of better understanding how we teach the Bible, the Bible's origins, and how we interpret meaning in the Bible.

To understand how Americans teach the Bible, I began examining Sunday school curriculum. What I found was that our earliest teaching of Scripture is approached from a literal perspective. For a moment, think about how confusing this would be for a child. They go home and watch a Pixar movie like *Onward*, and they inherently know that the movie is not true, but they come to church and hear that a big fish ate a man, and they are supposed to understand it as truth. Now I don't care who you are, but you must admit this creates quite the conundrum in the mind of an eight-year-old.

Personally, I am not suggesting that the Bible is full of make-believe stories; however, I am suggesting the delicate nature of teaching complex books to young children. Fortunately, our children love stories, and the origin of our Bible stems from a community of Jews that shared in this love of story.

When I graduated with my doctorate, my in-laws agreed to watch our three children and allow my wife and I to take a trip to New York City. Neither of us had been before, but we had heard our peers clamor about the magic of Times Square and the shows on Broadway. To be quite honest, I could care less about paying hundreds of dollars to see musicals, but as any good husband does, I went along for the ride. We saw *Wicked*, *Aladdin*, and even *The Office Musical Parody* (which if I was being honest I was very excited about). A singing Dwight sounded like great entertainment to me. Side bar: did you know that Netflix users streamed fifty-two billion minutes of *The Office* in a single year?

What is interesting about Broadway is its origin. You may not know this, but Broadway was started by Jews in an attempt to tell their stories. In recent years, PBS created an incredible documentary called *Broadway Musicals: A Jewish Legacy* that highlighted the Jewish origins of Broadway. Arguably, the American culture of the late twentieth century is distinctly Jewish due to the amount of Jewish filmmakers, authors, and the talent on Broadway during that era.

Within their oral society, Jews loved telling stories. This is evidenced in the pedagogical teaching of Jesus through the use of parables. For Jews, storytelling is a way of life. Even as Americans, we know that story carries with it power. I have been fortunate in my career to sit on an innovation in education committee for the Oklahoma governor. I also was invited to serve on a task force to help our governor rethink education for our state. I remember this task force spent days discussing the narrative we would share with the governor. We had pages of statistics and an overwhelming amount of educational research, but it was the stories of kids that would capture his heart.

Stories move and shape who we are and how we see life. My friend and colleague, Dr. Charles Rix, has his PhD in Hebrew Bible and his dissertation focused on Hebrew narrative. He has helped me develop a more holistic understanding of Scripture through first understanding the Hebrew culture and their way of life.

What I learned was that there is a significant tension between how the Hebrew culture found truth and how Westerners come to find truth. In many ways, this is due to the disconnect between an oral society and a literate society. Jewish culture was an oral society yet we have been living in what is called a literate society. Do you know some Americans actually argue over what wood Noah used to build the ark? Translations can't even agree on the wood debate. The New American Standard says gopher wood, and the New International Version says cypress wood. It's actually quite amusing to go into commentaries and read about the discrepancies in which wood it was and why scholars can't be certain.

To be honest, I have spent very little brain power on the wood debate primarily because I believe it doesn't matter nor did the Jews telling the story probably care what type of wood it was. This may be a silly example, but the point I am making is that oral societies tell stories, and like us, when we are telling stories, we often know the details are not the point of our story. Whether or not gopher or cypress wood was used doesn't take away from the larger truths of the story of Noah. However, in a literate society and within the context of American culture, details matter because we connect details to facts. To further that, we connect fact to truth hence the reason when there is a discrepancy in the details, we see it impacting truth. Jews were not concerned with preserving details, but they were passionate about communicating truth.

Remember the question that plagued me after the teacher felt she needed to defend the authority of Scripture? I have come to the painful realization that I don't think she needed to, and furthermore, by defending it, she created more of a wedge between her opportunity to witness to that student. Don't get me wrong; the authenticity of Scripture and the power of our God is critical. However, it may not need to be a starting point. What if we started from a more broad context? When a student articulates a question between their faith and the authenticity of Scripture, we shouldn't start by defending its authenticity. We must first get them thinking beyond themselves. We must ask them a question like do you think there is a world outside of the one your brain can comprehend? Or do you think there is a world beyond what you know? Ask questions that create larger narratives for them in their minds. Help them understand that their Western way of thinking may be limited.

While I personally believe Jesus fed five thousand people, it would prove nearly impossible to communicate this truth within the mind of a traditional Gen Zer. It's why we must start from a larger scope and begin helping them understand a world beyond their comprehension. At some point, we want to get them to understand the authenticity of Scripture and the real power of God. However, it's not the starting place but it's probably more like a finish line. As evidence of this, Barna in 2018 published their data in a book called *Gen Z*. In it they quoted a Gen Z student from one of their focus groups who said, "There is no such thing as truth, but there are facts. Not only can people believe whatever truth they want, there is always room for truth to change." It is evident that our children are growing up in a world where facts and truth are in competition with each other.

To further this conversation, let's stick with my Broadway theme and move to the show *Wicked* as the audience watches this heated discourse taking place between the Wizard and Elphaba. Elphaba had always wanted to meet the Wizard because she had such admiration for him only to find out that the Wizard had been a phony.

WIZARD. *I never asked for this/ Or planned it in advance / I was merely blown here/ By the winds of chance / I never saw myself / As a Solomon or Socrates / I knew who I was / One of your dime-a-dozen / Mediocrities / Then suddenly I'm here / Respected—worshiped even / Just because the folks in OZ / Needed someone to believe in / Does it surprise you / I got hooked, and all too soon? / What can I say? / I got carried away / And not just by a balloon… Wonderful / They called me "wonderful" / So I said "Wonderful, if you insist" / "I will be wonderful" / And they said "Wonderful" / Believe me its hard to resist / 'Cause it feels wonderful / They think I'm wonderful / Hey look who's wonderful / This corn-fed hick / who said: "it might be keen / To build a town of green / And a wonderful road of yellow brick!" / See, I never had a family of my own, I was always travelin'. So, I guess I just wanted to give the citizens of Oz everything.*
ELPHABA. *So you lied to them.*
WIZARD. *Only verbally. Besides, they were the lies they wanted to hear. The truth is not a thing of fact or reason / The truth is just what ev'ryone agrees on. Where I am from we believe all sorts of things that aren't true. We call it—"history."*

Ahhhh…the complexities of truth. Absolute truth. This has become the generational faith debate my entire life. "They just don't believe in absolute truth anymore," said every old man I have ever met. What makes something true? Does the fact that multiple people agree on something make it true? The tension between a literal view of Scripture and an oral view of Scripture causes older generations great angst because in their minds, it's a matter of truth. If you don't believe in the literalness of the Scriptures, then you don't believe in truth.

Well, another aspect to the way Jews told stories is that they understood truth in a more holistic way than a literate culture would find truth. Jews looked at truth like a cube. To them, there are many different sides and layers to truth. Let me unpack this statement a bit, and I want to start with the way Jews understood truth. As mentioned, Jews found truth from many perspectives. Since storytelling is such an innate part of their culture and dialogue, it is possible Jews would not be as concerned about whether or not something was true. Allow me to explain. They would argue that we shouldn't ask whether or not something is true; rather, we should ask how something is true. Do you see the difference between these questions?

Westerners tend to want to ask the question, "Is this true?" Asking whether or not something is true is not the only way to find truth. We must understand that there are different ways to find the truth. One way to find truth is to fact-check and find the historical significance. Another way to find the truth is to ask, "How is this true?" As Americans, this question makes us uncomfortable, but we do this all the time. We spend a significant portion of our lives reading stories or watching movies that portray truth in fictional ways. A simple biblical example of this would be the story of the prodigal son. The majority of Christians would argue that this story illustrates a deep truth about our God. With that said, I have never met a Christian or a scholar who wanted to know the mailing address of the prodigal son's home before they would believe the truth the story depicts. From a simplistic example like the prodigal son, it is easy for us all to grasp that truth can be found in the context of a fictional story. So from this perspective, fiction is not void of truth.

Let me ask you this: what is the truth of Genesis chapter 1? Is the truth in the literalness of a six-day creation, or does the truth lie in the fact that God is the Creator of the world? Can an oral reading of the creation account lead to the same truth as a literal reading? Let me remind you; this book does not serve as a commentary on Genesis chapter 1, yet this book is designed to help you navigate an understanding of Scripture in a way that creates a common ground between generational viewpoints of the Bible.

A teacher at the school I was superintendent of received a master's degree in storytelling. That might win the award for coolest master's degree ever. She believed that part of the disconnect between accepting the miracle stories of the Bible for Generation Z is the skepticism they have when data isn't available. They want proof, but the problem we have is that storytelling is fundamentally about *making meaning* when the meaning is somewhat ambiguous. Aboriginal natives in Australia believe that you never moralize stories because the story can have multiple meanings depending on the stage of life and circumstances you find yourself in. By ascribing meaning, you take away the opportunity of the individual to find new meanings.

Deborah Tannen, a linguist, said:

> By doing some of the work of making meaning, hearers or readers become participants in the discourse. In other words, they become meaningfully, mythically involved. I am suggesting, furthermore, that these two types of involvement are necessary for communication, and that they work, in part, by creating emotional involvement. It is a tenet of education that students understand information better, perhaps only, if they discover it for themselves rather than being told it. Much as one cares *for* a person, animal, place or object that one has taken care *of,* so listeners and readers not only understand information better but care more about it—understand it because they care about it—if they have worked to make it's meaning.

We can let students read about the miracles of Jesus, but making meaning from that story and being involved in it is what makes them care about the information. What does it mean to a student that he has no evidence for and no way to categorize a miracle? It means nothing because he needs to do the work to make meaning out of it. We must be willing to help students learn to make meaning and care about the stories of the Bible because it is part of faith development. So instead of first defending authenticity, let's first help them *make meaning* of the story. Much the same way that people used to listen to fairy tales and trust that there is a realm in which magic is real and strange things are possible, we have to find a way to teach our children to have the imagination necessary to believe that there is a Creator big enough to feed five thousand men and create a world to love us, even to the death of His own child.

As I close up this chapter I want to spend a little bit of time discussing some of the flaws of the literate culture. I want us all to know that no culture is perfect but especially a literate culture. As noted, many in the older generations want to start their teachings of Scripture with the inherency and the authority of Scripture which they would connect with a literate view of Scripture. They want younger generations to believe they are literate. I think we need to allow some humility here.

The Bible is an ancient text full of life and meaning. It is the most powerful book in existence and has impacted the lives of millions of people for centuries. The words on the pages are life altering and share the deepest truths in life. "Reading the Bible responsibly and respectfully today means learning what it meant for ancient Israelites to talk about God the way they did, and not pushing expectations on texts written long ago and far away," argued Dr. Peter Enns in his book, *The Bible Tells Me So*. It is crucial that we find ways to better engage younger generations through an understanding of the validity of these ancient texts. It is evident that generations are approaching this text in different ways, and this dissonance between how we approach Scripture creates an uncertainty in the sincerity of our Scriptures.

I grew up as a preacher's kid and received my undergraduate degree in biblical text. I have taken two years of Greek and a difficult semester of Hebrew. I will be the first to admit that these do not give me the credentials to be considered a biblical scholar. I know enough, however, to walk us through a basic understanding of some of the challenges we face when understanding the Scripture. It's important that we share this fundamental understanding of *making meaning* of Scripture because older generations are building up walls between our kids and the Bible based on the ways they come to understand these ancient texts.

First, let's begin with a basic grammar lesson. As you may know, our Old Testament text was not first written in English, rather Hebrew. So our text had to go through a translation process from Hebrew to English. Since I am no scholar, allow me to introduce you to Rabbi Magonet as he illustrates the potential grammatical concerns in our translations using Isaiah 1:18:

> Come, let us reason together, says the Eternal
> if your sins are as crimson,
> they shall be white as snow;
> if they are red as scarlet,
> they shall become like wool!

In this translation of the text, it would appear that God is offering an endless supply of forgiveness. But, and that is a big but, because based on the translation of the punctuation of the text, you could have an altogether opposite understanding of the text:

> Come let us reason together, says the Eternal.
> If your sins are as crimson,
> shall they be as white as snow?!
> If they are red as scarlet,
> shall they become like wool?!

As Westerners, we come to our English Bibles as foreigners to the text. We must acknowledge the intricacies of the text that we miss because of our cultural distance. Now expanding upon our *cultural distance*, I mentioned we lose even more in translation by moving from the original oral story of the text to a new written form of the text. There are some significant differences between our Western culture and the culture during the time of our earliest Scriptures. These differences can be found in the contrast between oral societies and literate societies. Scripture was written within the context of an oral society. Jews loved stories, and they valued truth telling through oral form. I can just imagine as a child sitting around listening to my father tell the stories of faith. The story of creation, the story of

Noah, the story of Moses, the story of David, and the many stories they had to tell.

As oral stories do, they may adapt over time, but the truth of the story is not the story itself, rather, the point the story is trying to make. Peter Enns suggested that as current readers of the Scriptures, we should listen to the ancient voice of the text because it is the voice of the narrative that is trying to convey its message to us. He explained, "The Bible—from back to front—is the story of God told from the limited point of view of real people living at a certain place and time."

In the Western world, older generations have lived within the framework of literacy. It is in a literate society that we began to develop the concept that the Bible was a history book which is a flawed Western narrative for how the Bible functions. It is evident that when the oral stories were put in written form, they began to change the way we think. Peter Enns argued that this history view of Scripture is a flawed approach when understanding its meaning:

> History is huge for the Christian faith. So, when the Bible says that such and such happened, the default response is to take it at face value as our kind of history. But the Bible itself complicates matters: its writers are clearly engaged in consciously shaping the past rather than simply reporting it.

The driving biblical question within the literate society is, did what happen in the Bible actually happen? Dr. Enns would argue, as well as a significant number of other scholars, that this is an irrelevant question.

To further explore this contextual issue, I want to look at the work of rabbi Dr. Jonathan Magonet. In his book *A Rabbi Reads the Bible*, he illustrates this concept through the telling of a story that started at a Soviet party where Stalin held up a telegram which he said he had just received from the disgraced Trotsky. "This is what he now confesses!" said Stalin and then he read, "I was wrong— stop— you were right—stop—you should be a leader—stop."

Rabbi Magonet expressed that at this point, the crowd erupted with applause, but as Stalin was about to sit down, a hand went up. A little old man stood up and said, "Pardon me, comrade Stalin, but I think you may have read the telegram incorrectly." Silence fell. Stalin said nothing and waited. "What comrade Trotsky actually meant to say was: I was wrong?!—stop—You were right?!—stop— You should be a leader?!?"

Rabbi Magonet would go on to say, "This story is particularly revealing because it mimics one of the fundamental problems about reading the Hebrew Bible—namely that the text itself is utterly lacking in what we would think of as punctuation." I love this quote by Rabbi Magonet regarding understanding the meaning of Scripture. "It is clearly absurd, let alone intellectually dishonest, to deny the possibilities of multiple readings." I suppose I am convinced that we must come to Scripture with a more humble approach when in dialogue with Generation Z.

"We are none of us objective readers of the text, we are only more or less conscious of the degree to which our reading is colored by our particular circumstances and the times in which we live," said Dr. Magonet.

In his book *Story as Torah*, Dr. Gordon Wendham argued:

> A text is essentially a message from an author to its first readers, which the author hoped would be understood and acted on. Because both readers and author shared a common language and culture, there was a reasonable chance that the writer's intentions would be realized and the message understood correctly. Our distance in time and space from the author and first readers makes it much more difficult to pick up the original sense of the message.

RAISING CONTRIBUTORS
IN A CULTURE OF CONSUMERISM AND SKEPTICISM

Simply stated, the Western culture is significantly different from the culture in which the Bible was written. That sounds like a very obvious statement, but often as we come to Scripture, we forget this. We have become so encultured into the normality of our lives we forget we bring a very Western viewpoint to Scripture. The tension this creates between what the Scripture is trying to do and how we receive the Word of God can be frustrating to say the least. However, more than this being a personal frustration for us, it can create a wedge between older and younger generations.

Consider for a moment the difference between hearing a story and reading a story.

Hearing a story	vs.	*Reading a story*
Story might change the next time you hear it		Story never changes
Story might be grammatically correct		Story has been edited for perfection
Nonverbal cues highlight the main points		Reader must assume main points
Truth can lie within story form		Truth lies within facts of the story

Peter Enns argued:

> Stories of the past differ because storytellers are human beings. No storyteller is all knowing about the past, but limited by his or her time and place, and the fact that no human sees every angle on everything. Stories also differ by what storytellers are consciously trying to do in their stories, what their takeaway is. They are not objective observers and don't pretend to be. They are artists bringing past and present together to

leave the audience with something to ponder, to persuade, to inspire.

It is critical to note that nothing I have said so far disagrees with the authority of our Scriptures. I am suggesting though that as we attempt to interpret these Scriptures, we may make some mistakes.

CHAPTER 7

What Is Real?

> I realize that it isn't very fashionable to talk about some things as being holy; nevertheless, if we ever want to rid ourselves of personal and corporate emptiness, brokenness, loneliness, and fear we will have to allow ourselves room for that which we cannot see, hear, touch, or control.
>
> —Mr. Rogers

I wrote most of this book tucked away in the corner of a cool coffee shop with free coffee refills. Sometimes it was a hip spot in our quaint little downtown; other times it was late into the night at a Denny's or IHOP. This chapter, however, was written mostly outside at a park near my house. The weather was great, so I found a quiet shady place in the middle of the park. As I write this, I am watching a summer camp full of kids from five to eight years old sitting on blankets around a camp counselor reading them a picture book. I can't make out what book it is, but I can tell it is a book with pictures and relatively few words as she reads a portion and then shows them the pages.

My first attempts at becoming an author was in the world of children's literature. I was working on my doctorate and thought I was going to do my dissertation on the concept of grit. Grit is an idea made popular by Dr. Angela Duckworth, and it focuses on hard work and not giving up. During my research at that time, I realized there were not many resources on teaching grit to children. So I embarked on an attempt to give the concept of grit a face, and I ended up publishing a children's book called *The Adventures of Grit*. I dedicated this book to my son who was three years old at the time.

Then my wife and I found out we were having twin daughters, so I felt obligated to write a picture book dedicated to them. I wanted it to be meaningful, so I published my second children's book that focused on self-worth and called it *The Diary of a Lousy Book*. My first book told the story of hard work amid times of adversity while my second book told the simple truth that beauty comes from within. Both of these books told make-believe stories that conveyed truths about life.

To understand make believe helps us better understand the *cultural distance* between oral and literate societies. First, we should examine more closely the role of story. Even since I was growing up in the 80s and 90s, it is clear that the way stories are told has significantly evolved. As a kid, I loved stories, but I hated reading; despised it actually. I was the kid that went to the book fair to buy a Michael Jordan, Britney Spears, or Alicia Silverstone poster (don't judge me). Some of my friends liked nonfiction-type books. For whatever reason, they seemed to be the smart kids. The others seemed to be drawn toward the fiction. I didn't like either, but if I was forced to read, I'd choose fiction. I remember liking *Stuart Little*, *Hatchet*, and *The Missing Face on the Milk Carton* series. Now I love to read, but I'm drawn toward nonfiction with this desire to acquire more knowledge.

It's in a literate culture where we see this distinction in the categories of stories. On a regular basis, my wife and I take our children to the public library, and what a great place it is to really understand the categorical differences between fiction and nonfiction. A literate culture knows that there is a difference in these categories. If I go to the fiction section, I will find mythical stories of fairy tales and wonderlands that take us to magical places. If I go over to the nonfiction section, I will learn of history, humanity, and the truths of life. An oral culture and the culture surrounding our Bible stories would not have created these bold categories; rather, they would have woven fiction and nonfiction through their narratives to communicate certain truths or ethics.

As I was researching the origins of fiction and nonfiction, I came across an interesting article written by Niels Ebdrup. The article is called "The Origin of Fiction":

> *Today we are perfectly aware that crime fiction and other novels are based purely on imagination. We know full well that characters like Harry Potter aren't real and that Sherlock Holmes and Dr Watson never actually walked the streets of London.*
>
> *However, had these books been published in the Middle Ages, their readers would have thought that the stories about Harry, Holmes and Watson were real—simply because there were books about them.*
>
> *New research reveals how our ancestors came up with the idea to tell tall tales in books.*
>
> *"In the Middle Ages, books were perceived as exclusive and authoritative. People automatically assumed that whatever was written in a book had to be true," says Professor Lars Boje Mortensen of the Institute of History and Civilization at the University of Southern Denmark.*
>
> *"Most people only knew the Bible, which was believed to tell the truth about the world. Because of this, it came as a big surprise when books full of fabrications first started to appear in the 12th century."*
>
> *Up until the High Middle Ages in the 12th century, books were surrounded by grave seriousness.*
>
> *The average person only ever saw books in church, where the priest read from the Bible. Because of this, the written word was generally associated with truth.*

The perception of books was no different among learned monks, who studied books about science and philosophy in the large monasteries of the Middle Ages.

The monks presumed that the descriptions of the paths of the planets and the human soul were ancient truths. Truths like the words of the Bible. The books read by the religious men had been passed on from generation to generation for centuries, and this meant that they acquired a special authority.

The practically religious relationship with books started to change gradually at the end of the 12th century—and has continued to change ever since.

In the library, fiction is kept separate from non-fiction. We generally expect a work of non-fiction about dwarves to tell us some facts about why some people are born smaller than others.

If, on the other hand, we go to the fiction section and pick up a volume of the Lord of the Rings series, we'd get an entirely different take on the topic.

In Tolkien's imaginary world, dwarves are a separate race. But we don't mind. When we read fiction, we expect to be entertained by a good story, and because of that we accept that the novel we are reading deviates from accepted fact. This is due to a tacit agreement between the author and the reader—an invisible contract of sorts.

"We can only understand something as fiction if an 'invisible contract' has been formed between author and reader beforehand. A contract that says: 'this is only make-believe'," says Mortensen.

"The same rule applies when we go to the cinema to see a movie like Batman. There we as the audience have a 'contract' with the director stating

> *that the superhero doesn't exist in reality, but that we will pretend that he does during the movie."*
>
> *The 'invisible contract' between writers of fiction and their readers first appeared in the Middle Ages. The new study shows that the contract materialized over the course of several centuries. It all started a few hundred years after the death of Jesus, when it became common practice to think up continuations of the events in the Bible and write them down as truth.*
>
> *Christians in the Middle Ages and antiquity didn't feel that the Bible provided them with all the answers they were looking for. The great book offers a lot of information about the life of Jesus, but there are also gaps in the descriptions, such as when the Son of God returns to Earth after his death and stays there for almost 40 days.*
>
> *"Some started to wonder: why doesn't it say anything much about what Jesus actually said, when he returned to Earth? People started to think up answers to that. They filled in the gaps in the Bible by writing so-called apocryphal gospels as a supplement. In other words, they used their imagination to fill in the gaps," says the researcher.*

Fiction and nonfiction were not on the radar in the culture that Jesus lived in, and put simply, Jesus wasn't an author. Have you ever realized that we have no example of Jesus writing anything down? For that matter, we have no example of Jesus telling His disciples to take notes. In my American-educated brain, I could easily see Jesus standing up among a semicircle of disciples around him with Jesus saying, "Write this down. You'll want to remember this one."

My millennial self believes that thought leaders are content creators. At least, they are today, but Jesus wasn't an author; He was an orator. Jesus could have been the greatest content creator of all time. He loved stories and saw the power in teaching truth through oral narrative. Perhaps instead of a book, Jesus could have had His stories go viral on YouTube or a podcast about loving your neighbor. We love the stories of Jesus even though some of them have many cultural nuances that we do not naturally understand. Regardless, we still love the fact that He taught through story.

Stories flood the pages of our Scriptures, and Generation Z struggles to grasp the function story plays in these inspired pages. As Generation Alpha begins to age and start studying Scripture at deeper levels, I am afraid they will too. Let's go back to the story of Jennifer struggling to understand the miracle story of Jesus feeding the five thousand or the class that struggled to understand the story in Revelation. As adults, we know that these two stories are very different types of literature, and we know that they are doing different things in our Holy Scripture. However, most of our kids come to the text believing it is a nonfiction book. Maybe we unintentionally taught them that the Bible is nonfiction (because we believe it to be true), or maybe we actually intentionally taught them this. Regardless, the Bible is difficult to understand within the constraints of fiction and nonfiction.

In a certain way, Pixar has also formed our children's minds toward a deep understanding of the fairy-tale world which has created a disenchantment for the miracles found in the Scriptures.

Pixar further led this generation to a firm distinction between fictional and nonfictional life. Pixar, through their exquisite storytelling and their larger-than-life characters, has been able to create a significant divide between the two genres of fiction and nonfiction. For the Jews, storytelling was just a way of life. If you wanted to convey a truth, you would depict it from a story as seen through the parables of Jesus. Today, built into their core worldview, our children believe that there is a fictional world and a nonfictional world. To take this a step further, it has developed a mindset that fictional activity is in conflict with our nonfictional world because fiction and nonfiction are distinct concepts.

The Bible, as I know it, does not have to fall under a categorical selection of fiction or nonfiction. These are terms and understandings that have surfaced rather recently in human history; therefore, I am okay with the Bible sitting outside the bounds of this very Western categorical framework. At the end of the day, the Bible does not have to fit into my American understanding, and I should give the Bible the freedom it needs to teach me the deeper truths of God in its own ancient way. The Word of God is a cosmic work created before the beginning of time, and one way it manifests itself is through the ink on our pages. So Jesus wasn't a fiction or nonfiction author; He was simply a magnificent storyteller. Storytelling in itself has been around since the beginning as we know it. Over time, we have witnessed storytelling evolve and morph through different modalities and styles.

Today, we are entering an age where story has taken over our devices and is leading us into a new virtual age. So where does Generations Alpha and Z fit into this literate society we have spent so much time discussing? It's very clear that Generation Alpha is charting a new path forward. They are leading us out of a literate society and into a visual society. Dr. Ong would call this new territory a *secondary orality* as he stated:

> Our understanding of the differences between orality and literacy developed online in the electronic age, not earlier. Contrasts between electronic media and print have sensitized us to the earlier contrast between writing and orality. The electronic age is also an age of 'secondary orality', the orality of telephones, radio, and television.

Did you know that according to Common Sense Media, when Generation Z was asked about the activities they enjoyed, they reported these statistics:

- 73 percent said listening to music
- 45 percent said watching TV
- 45 percent said watching online videos
- 42 percent said playing video games
- 36 percent said social media

So there is no doubt we have lived in secondary orality. It is very possible that secondary orality has even developed since Dr. Ong first coined the term, and Generation Alpha has invited us to move into a visual society. In many ways, the transition of our world since Scripture could look something like this.

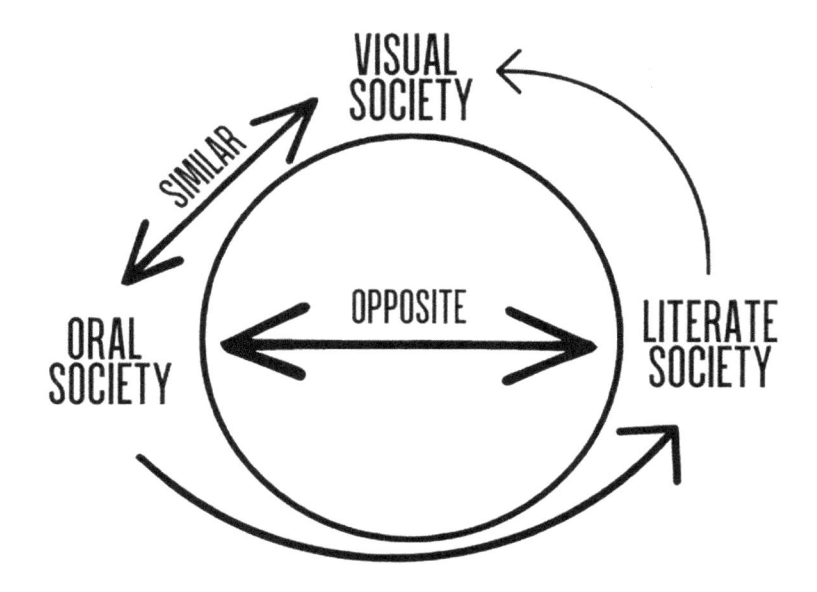

```
           VISUAL
           SOCIETY
      SIMILAR ↗       ↘
   ORAL  ←  OPPOSITE  →  LITERATE
   SOCIETY                SOCIETY
```

This image depicts how we have moved from oral to literate, and these two societies are distinctly different. As we transition into this new visual society, we are actually being drawn closer to the heartbeat of an oral society where story, narrative, and image are valued. Images looked different in the context of Moses let's say, but it was evident that images played a significant role. Think about the power of statues, idols, and signs that were used all throughout the Old Testament. Even one of our most used passages on faith development highlighted the value of image as Deuteronomy 6 stated, "Tie them as symbols on your hands and bind them on your foreheads. Write them on the doorframes of your houses and on your gates."

Images were deeply meaningful to God's people. Another example is when God's people were instructed to raise an Ebenezer, a stone of remembrance, in important locations where God helped His people. It was simply a physical image to help them remember the important, life-changing events. Seeing these stones would remind them of God's faithfulness and help them make decisions with God's faithfulness in mind.

Images and media among our new generations are rapidly changing communication. Through social media, GIFs, and the iPhone camera, we are starting to see a generation communicate almost entirely by picture or video. We are watching a major social shift taking place, and we must recognize its impact on culture, faith, and our understanding of truth. In many ways, the similarities in this new visual era and the oral society are overwhelming. According to a strategy and design company called UD:

> One of the most striking differences between Millennials and Generation Z would have to be their choice and method of communication. Gen Z communicates with images and they multitask across five screens as opposed to millennials preferring to communicate on two screens and via text. Gen Z's attention spans are getting shorter as well, explaining their preference for video and images rather than text. They are the ultimate consumers of snack media. They communicate in bite sizes. Punchy headlines or razor sharp text resonate much better than lengthy chunks of words or long winded passages. They communicate in symbols. They speak in emoticons and emojis. The symbols provide context and create subtext for their private conversations. Text has effectively been replaced by images.

They go on to boldly say, "The alphabet is so twentieth century." They do not even talk with a full alphabet anymore since so many abbreviations have taken the place of appropriate spelling. IDK, ILU, BRB, and LOL are just a few of the hundreds of new abbreviations we use to communicate today. To that end, abbreviations are now being replaced with memes and short videos. Generations Alpha and Z might be the first Westernized generation to have a grasp on what the Jews were doing during the time of Scripture. The love of story is awakening this generation and potentially could be a way to bring this group of children back into the faith landscape.

I firmly believe that if Jesus had the ability to use actual images in His teaching, He would have. Jesus was a master at painting images with His words as a way of teaching. However, to reclaim the intent of narrative within the oral society for Generations Alpha and Z, we must be willing to come to Scripture differently. Currently, I see the generational gap in approaching scripture like this:

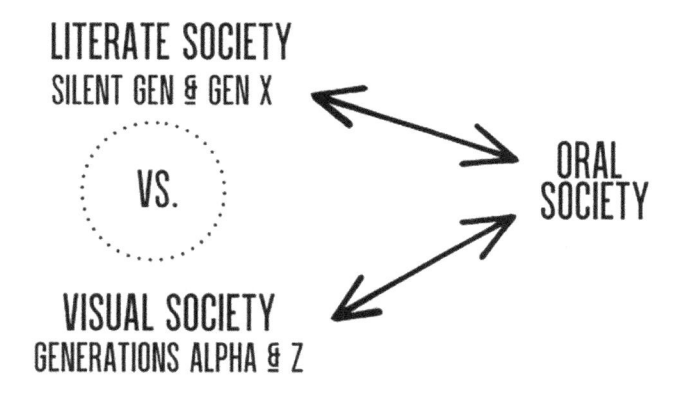

LITERATE SOCIETY
SILENT GEN & GEN X

VS.

ORAL SOCIETY

VISUAL SOCIETY
GENERATIONS ALPHA & Z

Older generations are trying to understand Scripture through the lenses of their literate society. This also means that they are trying to teach Scripture to Generation Z through this same lens. The disconnect is that Generations Alpha and Z are operating within the framework of a distinctly different society and framework which is creating quite the tension. Jennifer's example of being in class and listing her *how* questions related to Jesus's miracle is a direct reflection of this disconnect. Let me remind you that Mrs. Johnson's reaction was to defend the validity of the story.

Older generations often view Scripture as a history book or rule book. Peter Enns argued, "Many Christians have been taught that the Bible is truth downloaded from heaven, God's rulebook, a heavenly instructional manual—follow the directions and out pops a true believer." He went on to suggest in his book, *The Bible Tells Me So*, that "rather than a rulebook, the Bible is more like a land we get to hike through and explore its many paths and terrains. The land is both inviting and inspiring, but also unfamiliar, odd, and at points unsettling—even risky and precarious."

How do we navigate this tension? Well first, the older generations must humble themselves in their approach to Scripture and allow the oral narrative of Scripture to breathe and take shape within the minds of our kids. Attempting to prove that Jonah actually slept inside the stomach of a big fish will not benefit anyone and in fact will fall on deaf ears. Instead, a much better approach is to first invite them into the amazing story of God's people and allow them to first make meaning of the story. If we agree that we are transitioning out of a literate society, we must be aware that Generations Alpha and Z will be unable to comprehend a teaching of Scripture through a literate means. If you are going to take a literal approach of understanding Scripture with this generation, you will eventually lose because their minds are unable to process this understanding. They are able to see through the lens of science that the world wasn't created within six days.

Peter Enns explained it in this way:

> We understand today that the physical universe is bigger and older and operates very differently than how the biblical writers, and all other ancient people, thought. Many Christians stumble over this, thinking they are showing respect for the bible and obeying God by making the biblical story mesh with modern science, or rejecting modern science entirely in favor of God's word.

He went on to say:

> When ancient Isrealites wrote as they did about the physical world, they were expressing

their faith in God in ways that fit their understanding. It shouldn't get our knickers in a twist to admit that, from a scientific point of view, they were wrong. That doesn't make their faith, or the God behind it less genuine.

Believe it or not, I find this to be great news. We should be chartering different ways to interpret the words of text, and we should align our teaching of scripture much more closely to understanding it through an oral tradition. Instead of targeting each word and *piece of wood* in the text, we should be inviting them into participating in the amazing story of Scripture. We should be calling them to start living in the narrative shape of the gospel and helping them understand that truth is found in the Creator God, His Son on this earth, and that we will one day spend eternity with Him because of the resurrection.

I align myself to Peter Enns' view that "over the years I have grown more and more convinced that 'storytelling' is a better way of understanding what the bible is doing with the past than 'history writing.'"

CHAPTER 8

Demons, Ghosts, and Magic

> When I say it's you I like, I'm talking about that part of you that knows that life is far more than anything you can ever see or hear or touch. That deep part of you that allows you to stand for those things without which humankind cannot survive. Love that conquers hate, peace that rises triumphant over war, and justice that proves more powerful than greed.
>
> —Mr. Rogers

To stick with our theme of storytelling, allow me to remind some of you of a frightening movie that hit the big screen in 2005. It's arguably the scariest movie I have ever seen. *The Exorcism of Emily Rose* is about a young lady that had an exorcism of demonic possession. The question the movie highlights is an interesting one. Did Emily have a demon, or was it just a psychological issue? When I speak to large groups, typically in Christian settings, I like to ask this question. Did Emily have a demon, or was it something else? Typically, the room is full of people who believe she had a psychological issue. Very few believe it was demonic possession. However, for most of human history, and even currently in many parts of our world, demonic activity would never be questioned. So the second cultural phenomenon in the lives of Generations Alpha and Z is that the American Christian's belief in the mystical or transcendent is fading away.

In John 12:29, we see two different types of people. One group heard the voice of God, and the other group heard thunder. What group would you be in? Statistically, American Christians would hear thunder because our ears are not attuned to the mystical voice of God. Charles Taylor's work has led the conversation within this debate. Dr. Taylor in his book *A Secular Age* argued that there have been three distinctive eras in which we have lived. He called these Secular One, Secular Two, and Secular Three. Each of these eras played a significant role in how we experience or understand God. I am pretty certain that Dr. Taylor would be offended at my dumbed down version of his highly intellectual work, but this is how I understand it.

Secular One was an era where the sacred and secular were distinct. If you wanted to experience God, you would have to go to a sacred place and meet with a sacred person. That sacred person could then communicate to God on your behalf. As we transitioned into Secular Two, we then saw that the sacred and the secular danced with one another. It was during this time that we learned that you could experience God anywhere, even in the mall. Andrew Root in his book *The Pastor in a Secular Age* explained, "The Protestant Reformation made each person responsible for his or her own being before a Holy God. All were taught to read the Bible for themselves, given the keys to drive their own faith." He went on to say, "With the piestic desire to give everyone direct access to the vehicle of salvation, the bold line between the sacred and secular became much thinner."

Secular Three is a time where the sacred begins to slip away, and the secular begins to take over more of our lives. It is in Secular Three where the believability of God begins to fade, and our understanding of the transcendent begins to disappear. An important understanding of human belief patterns in Secular Three is the concept that we can fully flourish without a God.

After I began to critically think about Secular Two and Three, I began to ask myself, "Where do I think our kids are really at?" At first, I believed they probably lived in Secular Two because in all honesty, as a millennial, I found myself here much of the time. However, as I dug into the generational research, I learned that there was not much statistical data in the market to help me understand

RAISING CONTRIBUTORS IN A CULTURE OF CONSUMERISM AND SKEPTICISM

this more broadly. So I began down my own road of research, and it was interesting.

Way back in 2005, Dr. Christian Smith in his book *Soul Searching* coined the concept moralistic therapeutic deism (MTD). They argued that this was the theology of the younger generation. Here's the quick summary of MTD: students believed there is a God, this God was not actively working in the world, and they only went to God when they needed something. God was seen more like a therapist in the sky. This theology made so much sense to me as a millennial myself because at the time, I would have said I was a deist. I also remember listening to church leaders talk about how scary this was and how sad of a theology this was.

As I think of moralistic therapeutic deism, my mind reminisces back to childhood learning to align my brain to the Disney-like narratives of my childhood. The 1992 Disney hit *Aladdin* was one of those narratives I grew up with. I am sure you are familiar with the story. The story depicts a young humble Middle Eastern boy meeting a magical genie and getting to become a prince who marries the princess. It's a great story and the Genie on Broadway really steals the show. The question that had been plaguing me was this: had these Genie-type characters begun to create a new image of God's nature and character within the minds of children?

Take this exchange between Aladdin and the Genie after they met each other for the first time.

GENIE. *Genie! Of! The Lamp! Right here direct from the lamp, right here for your enjoyment wish fulfillment. Thank youuuuu!*
ALADDIN. *Whoa! Wish fulfillment?*
GENIE. *Three wishes to be exact. And ix-nay on the wishing for more wishes. That's it—three. Uno, dos, tres. No substitutions, exchanges or refunds.*
ALADDIN. *Now I know I'm dreaming.*
GENIE. *Well Ali Baba had them forty thieves. Scheherazadie had a thousand tales. But master you in luck 'cause up your sleeve. You got a brand of magic never fails! You got some power in your corner now. Some heavy ammunition in your camp. You got some punch, piz-*

zazz, yahoo and how. See all you gotta do is rub that lamp. And I'll say, "Mister Aladdin sir... What will your pleasure be? Let me take your order, jot it down. You ain't never had a friend like me. No no! Life is your restaurant. And I'm your maitre d'! C'mon whisper what it is you want. You ain't never had a friend like me. Yes sir, we pride ourselves on service. You're the boss, the king, the shah! Say what you wish, it's yours! True dish. How about a little more Baklava? Try some of column 'A.' Try all of column 'B.' I'm in the mood to help you dude. You ain't never had a friend like me. Can your friends do this? Do your friends do that? Do your friends pull this out their little hat. Can your friends go poof! Well looky here... Can your friends go Abracadabra, let 'er rip. And then make the sucker disappear? So don't you sit there slack jawed, buggy eyed. I'm here to answer all your midday prayers. You got me bona fide, certified. You got a genie for a change? D'affairs! I got a powerful urge to help you out... So what you wish I really want to know. You got a wish that's three miles long, no doubt. So all you gotta do is rub like so, and oh! Mister Aladdin, sir, have a wish or two or three. I'm on the job, you big nabob. You ain't never had a friend, never had a friend...like me!

MTD is a type of God that is very genie-like. A deity up in the sky waiting to fulfill your wishes. The ask-and-you-will-find type of a god. In MTD, God is a big happy therapist in the sky. Just say a prayer and poof, there is a god waiting in the sky ready to answer your prayers and hear you as you call upon him when you're in distress. God is waiting up there to grant your needs and your deepest wishes.

Dr. Smith called our kids moralistic therapeutic deists in 2005, but today, our kids are slipping further from deism into a world of disbelief. So while the millennial generation may have been considered more deistic in nature, Generation Z is shifting to an agnostic state. For them, plain and simply put, the whole God thing is just hard to believe. I primarily believe this because I see the believability of God slipping away. At least with MTD we had a group of kids that could acknowledge there was a God.

RAISING CONTRIBUTORS
IN A CULTURE OF CONSUMERISM AND SKEPTICISM

We are losing grasp of the certainty of God. I researched over 1,600 high school students from predominantly Christian schools with 96 percent of the population identifying themselves as Christian. What I found was startling. Here are some charts that support the fact that we are moving into disbelief.

I BELIEVE GOD IS ACTIVELY WORKING IN THE WORLD...

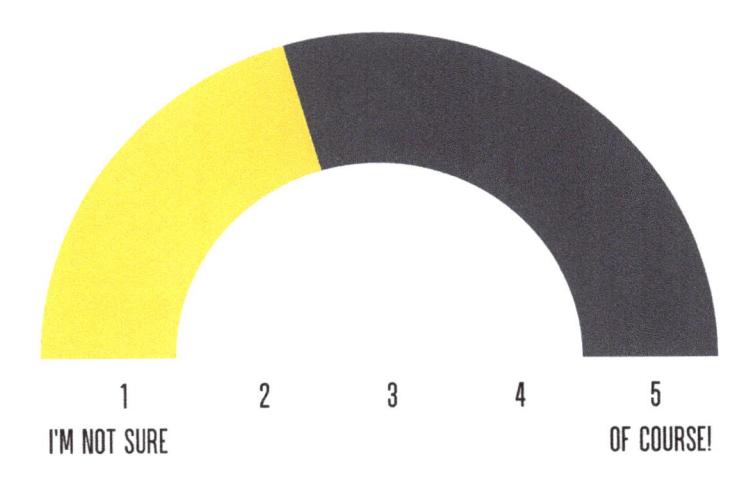

1 — I'M NOT SURE
2
3
4
5 — OF COURSE!

I BELIEVE IN THE ONE GOD OF THE BIBLE, YAHWEH...

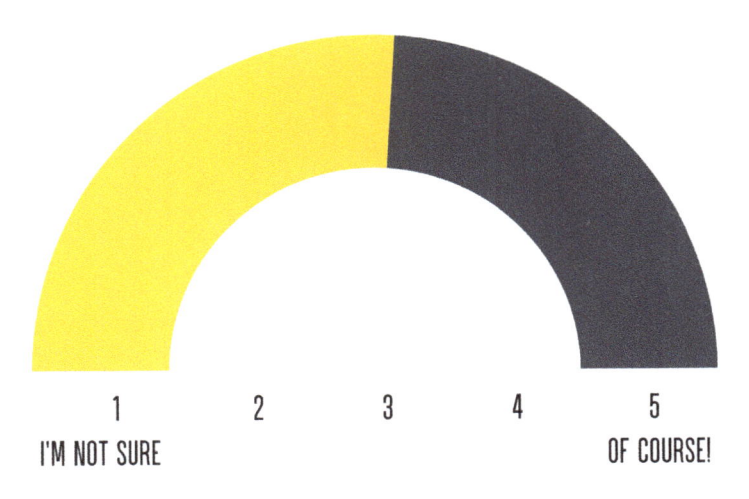

1 — I'M NOT SURE
2
3
4
5 — OF COURSE!

I BELIEVE THE BIBLE ORIGINATED FROM GOD AND GIVEN TO MEN TO WRITE...

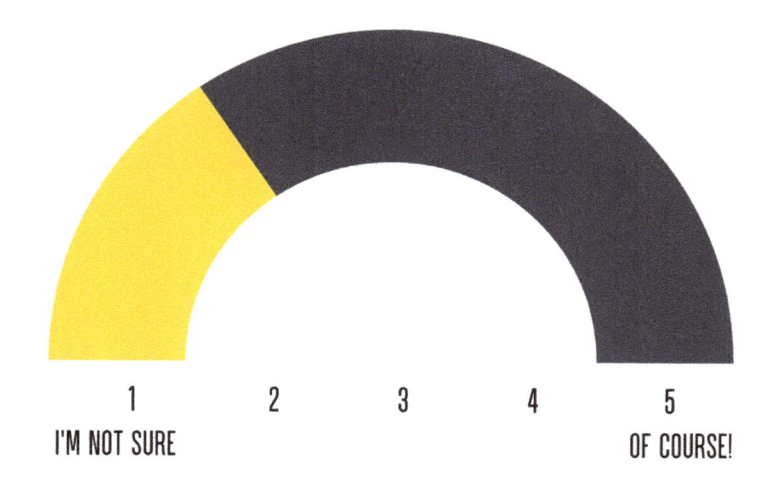

1 — I'M NOT SURE
2
3
4
5 — OF COURSE!

IT'S EASY FOR ME TO BELIEVE IN THE MIRACLES STORIES OF THE BIBLE...

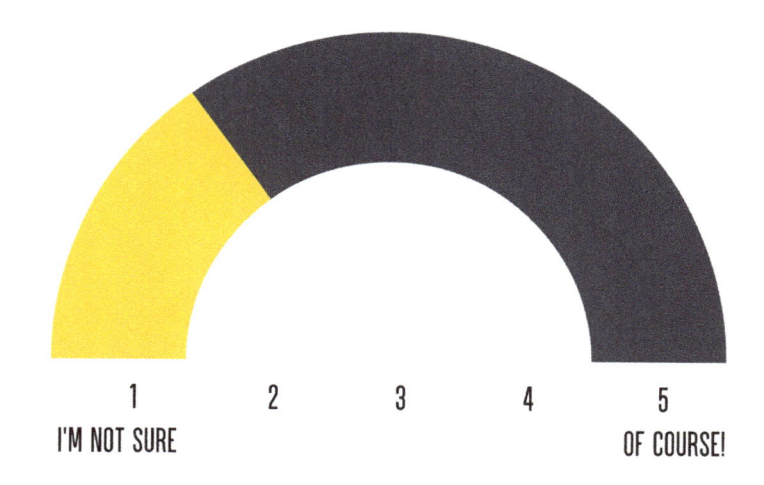

1 — I'M NOT SURE
2
3
4
5 — OF COURSE!

Let's attempt to see the faith landscape in which our kids are living. From my experiences working with youth and from the experiences of my peers in ministry, we tend to hear the same questions. Putting those questions into the context of this research and in

RAISING CONTRIBUTORS
IN A CULTURE OF CONSUMERISM AND SKEPTICISM

Secular Three, I now understand their origins. Those that work with Generation Z are hearing questions or phrases like this:

- *Do you think Jesus actually fed five thousand?*
- *Did Jonah really get swallowed by a big fish?*
- *Did creation actually happen in six days?*
- *Did God actually kill all those people in the Old Testament? If so, how could God do that?*
- *Is God real?*
- *Why do we leave some things out of the Scriptures and insist on other things?*
- *Is the Bible real?*

Now, Generation Z can't claim ownership of these questions. I am sure most Christians have asked these or similar questions throughout time. However, Generation Z are asking these questions in a very different culture than the one that many of us grew up in, and this is where a deeper tension lies. Within the context of a rational Western way of thinking, the believability in the transcendent is hard to grasp. I think we can know a lot about what to expect from Generation Alpha as we see the types of questions that Gen Z are asking. To go back to the illustration of Emily Rose, I like to use Mark 5:1–8.

> *They went across the lake to the region of the Gerasenes. When Jesus got out of the boat, a man with an impure spirit came from the tombs to meet him. This man lived in the tombs, and no one could bind him anymore, not even with a chain. For he had often been chained hand and foot, but he tore the chains apart and broke the irons on his feet. No one was strong enough to subdue him. Night and day among the tombs and in the hills he would cry out and cut himself with stones. When he saw Jesus from a distance, he ran and fell on his knees in front of him. He shouted at the top of his voice, "What*

> *do you want with me, Jesus, Son of the Most High God? In God's name don't torture me!" For Jesus had said to him, "Come out of this man, you impure spirit!"*

Here it is evident that Jesus is dealing with demon possession, but imagine for a second that yesterday, you were an eyewitness to this scene at your local mall. You're standing outside of the food court with your children, and you see a man running with their clothes ripped off, yelling at the top of his lungs and cutting himself with rocks. The security is trying to contain him and trying to put in handcuffs, but no man can contain him, not even the taser guns that are hitting him.

Now pause and let me ask you a simple question. At this moment, are you more likely to think this man is either on drugs or is mentally ill, or are you more likely to think this man is possessed by a demon? As I have posed this question to thousands of people across the country, I have only found a handful of individuals brave enough to raise their hand for demon possession. I do believe more people want to acknowledge demon possession, but the fact that they don't highlights how culturally unacceptable it is to admit to demon possession. For all practical purposes, everyone attaches drug use or mental illness to this scenario. Dr. Root argued:

> The immanent framing of the mental health industry wins us a leisure that our ancestors never could have imagined, as do fire trucks, pesticides, and State Farm insurance, The downpour of demons is over. The clouds have broke, and we can finally relax and let our hair down because we now assume that devils and omens don't exist.

He continued:

> The downpour of demons is so over that we pay sixteen dollars to be frightened in cinemas,

or line up to be startled in Halloween haunted houses. The horror movie becomes a recovery of a lost experience, or better, a lost worldview. We enter the theater to slide again into an enchanted world… Our ancestors would have found this form of entertainment shocking. They didn't need movies; they lived in an enchanted world where demons lurked. Everyday their lives were filled with frightening meaning.

How do we help our children fall in love with God when they live within this cultural context of disbelief in the transcendent even among Christians?

We struggle to understand the concept of a spiritual world that exists around us. I was recently visiting a different church, and the preacher had a great lesson that I am afraid went over the heads of his listeners. I am not suggesting that the church could not understand the content intellectually, but I do not think that the church felt the preacher's desired practical intent. Essentially this was the sermon. When you are in the middle of a battle, be it conflict, bad health, job loss, or other physical problems, we must remember that the battle is not against flesh and blood but rather the spiritual forces of our world. While this concept is biblical and aligns itself with the narrative of text, it does not register to a group of people living in the midst of Secular Three.

Now, if I were to poll a group of Christians and ask, "Do you believe in spiritual warfare?", I would anticipate there being a high level of Christians saying yes. And while we may intellectually think this, there is nothing in how we do life that would suggest that we actually believe this. Dr. Andrew Root in his book *The Pastor in a Secular Age* explained:

> Even today, in nearly every Christian tradition, the pastor stands before the people each week, offering in one way or another a web of arcane mysteries and liturgies, and asserts that

things are more than can be seen. Holding simple bread and wine, the pastor claims that it becomes something more. Dripping water on bodies or dipping full bodies in water, the pastor claims that there is something mysterious, even transformational happening. And some people are kind enough to concur, wishing their children to be baptized and finding some personal meaning in communion... People are willing to have their children baptized but are pretty sure that the tap water has no power or force to bring life out of death. Willing to happily take the bread and wine, hearing the words' this body broken for you,' they also know that it is store bought.

It's as if ministers in previous generations were able to use this spiritual warfare as a trump card, but our current generation is stuck in a place of disbelief only able to help further human flourishing in their communities.

When you understand this as our faith climate, it makes sense to see statistics like this from Barna, "Gen Z students are at least twice as likely as American adults to identify as atheist." From a larger perspective, it also makes sense to see how Gen Z and millennial Muslims are leaving Islam at the same rates as Gen Z and millennial Christians because transcendence in general is fading away in society. A lack of believability is the age in which we are living and attempting to spiritually form our children. Generation Alpha has been born into a culture that has little space for the believability of transcendence.

As we have moved throughout history in and out of different cultures, understandings, and frameworks, we become further removed from the heartbeat of our ancient texts and the story of God. We become formed and shaped by the culture in which we live, and unfortunately, we live during a time of the formation of the known and seen. It's why when my four-year-old son asked me to define real, I froze because I knew the theological impact of my answer to that question as we live in the here and now. My instinct was to say, "Well, real is what we see, touch, smell, and hear. Things like this truck and that tree, those are real." But as I quickly processed my answer, I thought of it in terms of our lack of believability in the transcendent and attempted to frame my answer differently. "Well, bud, there are many things that are real. You know when you are happy? That's a real feeling. Do you know when you are sad? That's a real feeling. God is real, Jesus is real. Real are things that are true."

Now I know my four-year-old in this moment was not able to process anything I had just said. But it was important to me that my son understood the concept of reality beyond his American understanding. Personally, I believe in the transcendent world of spiritual warfare, but I can't come close to comprehending this world. The good news is that this isn't a world that needs to be comprehended beyond the acknowledgment of its existence. It's the ability for each of us to believe in something bigger than ourselves that is the starting point to allow spiritual formation to take root. Knowing all of this, we are left with the question, now what? If we live in this world, how do we spiritually form our kids?

CHAPTER 9

So What Now?

> We all have different gifts, so we all have different ways of saying to the world who we are.
>
> —Mr. Rogers

Two of my favorite things in life are aquariums and zoos. My favorite aquarium is the Georgia Aquarium located in downtown Atlanta. My favorite zoo is in Omaha, Nebraska. When my wife and I were dating, I lived in Nebraska, and she lived in Texas. She would fly into Omaha to visit me, and we would go explore the Omaha Zoo. The indoor zoo exhibits there are amazing, and as an added bonus, they have an incredible aquarium. The bears and lions are some of my favorites to watch because of their powerful and distinctive nature.

Usually in their habitats, or you might call them cages, you will see trails that have been areas of the ground worn out over time because of their patterns of movement in the cage. Have you ever stood in front of one of the exhibits at the zoo and thought to yourself, *Something is wrong here.* This animal just seems depressed. If you have, you might be on to something. You see, there is this interesting behavior that animals often do when they are caged. They will pace back and forth, back and forth. If you watch it long enough, they could do this for hours at a time. There is a common term for this called *zoochosis*. Zoochosis is the repetitive, variant behavior patterns with no obvious goal or function. This behavior only happens to an animal that is in captivity. Why is this? More than likely, it is because these wild animals are not designed to live in a cage.

So let's think about our kids for a second. Are our children meant to live in the captivity of our protection, or are they meant to be empowered to bear God's image in the world? Are we allowing our children to grow, develop, and be nurtured in a healthy environment, or are we caging them up in ways where they can't blossom into the types of faithful adults they need to be? Many of our children are passive beings that are formed into a twenty-first-century cultural view of the world that cannot allow them to be the person God fully wants them to be. Let me remind you: Generation Alpha is the first generation where 100 percent of them have been born in the twenty-first century.

Our kids were not designed to be living in the cages of the twenty-first century. They are not made to live in cages of protection or the cage of the digital age. We know the twenty-first century is not the perfect training environment for image bearers. More likely, the original garden may have been the most idyllic of places to develop our God-given humanity. However, we can't transport back in time to the Genesis garden through the Minecraft transportal. We can't move away from the city and build compounds to hide from our lived reality. So we must figure out a way to live in this cultural moment and raise contributors.

First, we must help our children feel connected to their Creator. During my research of 1,600 Gen Zers, I uncovered an interesting statistic related to students' feelings of their connectedness to God. When asked what their feelings of how closely connected they were to God, the findings showed a decline from sixth grade to twelfth grade.

Gen Z | Feels Closely Connected to God

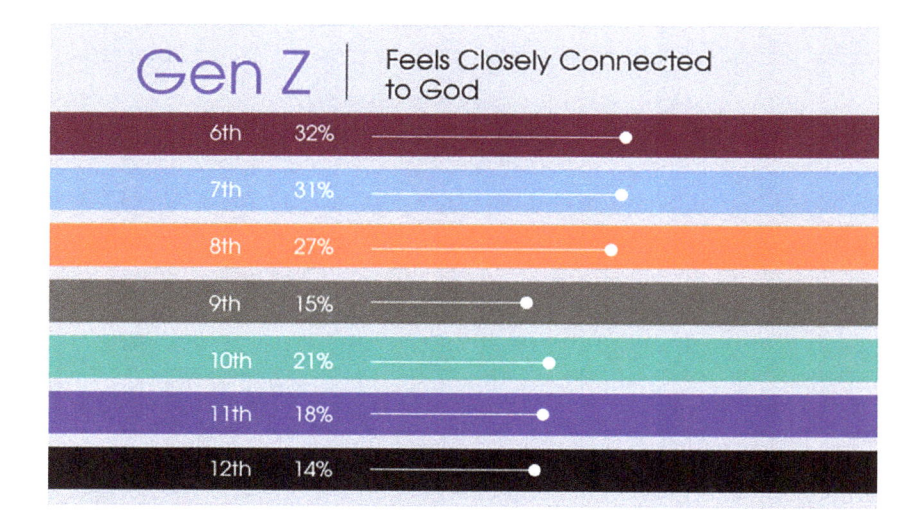

Grade	Percentage
6th	32%
7th	31%
8th	27%
9th	15%
10th	21%
11th	18%
12th	14%

Let's consider some of the potential reasons for this finding. Are we building a strong spiritual foundation in elementary? Is our elementary faith formation more knowledge focused or heart focused? Typically, what we find in Sunday school and children's ministries at churches are a series of Old Testament lessons that are watered down and not fully accurate depictions of Hebrew narratives. They sing cute songs of the destruction of the flood or other adult events of the Old Testament, and we then expect this to transform their hearts to love God. I am not sure we are being intentional in faith formation at the children's ministry level.

We can raise children who know God but don't love God. We must be intentional in raising children whose hearts do not fall in love with things of our culture but rather use their hearts to navigate this culture through the lens of their faith. I look forward to the day when my children will be able to read a book to me at night, but I long for the day that they use their hearts as a compass to align their actions with those of Jesus.

As an academic leader who is committed to the formation of the next generation of students, it's important that I understand effective teaching strategies. One important strategy when working with children is found in Bloom's taxonomy. This well-known model takes a student from remembering content to creating content. It is a learning model and best practice that educators use to help their students develop critical thinking skills. To move up the pyramid from lower-order thinking (simply remembering and understanding facts) to higher-order thinking (analysis, evaluation, creation), we must push, challenge, and create opportunities for critical thinking. I think parents and children's ministry leaders could learn from Bloom.

In this method of teaching, teachers attempt to guide students from consuming knowledge to contributing this knowledge to others in practical ways. Academics have been using Bloom's for years. It is interesting to see how little strategies like Bloom's have been woven into the fabric of children's ministries. So many of our children's ministry strategies are focused on lower-level thinking strategies like memorization.

An important goal when cultivating contributors isn't that they remember biblical content, rather, that students learn to contribute to society in meaningful ways using what they have been taught. This is the outcome of an impactful education. Bloom's taxonomy should go beyond the academic classroom into youth groups, families, summer camps, and any experience desiring to reach and mold our kids.

Forming the hearts of our children must take intentionality. As I was thinking about the value of Bloom's taxonomy for education, I began to think about the work of Dr. James K.A. Smith on formation and started down a path of connecting these two concepts. What I created was centered around liturgical taxonomies. In his work, Dr. Smith discusses how we must go through periods where we calibrate our hearts. In my mind, information does not form us. I am not suggesting that information is not important, but I am devaluing its role within the formation of our hearts. As I have mentioned, I think experiences, or as Dr. Smith suggests, liturgies, shape who we are.

So take a look at this illustration. This figure shows how information provides us a baseline in which to start, but our hearts are being shaped in a higher order way through the experiences in which we live. There are moments in time where our hearts must be recalibrated to realign with our Creator, so a transformation process happens. This is the life cycle of faith.

Liturgical Taxonomy

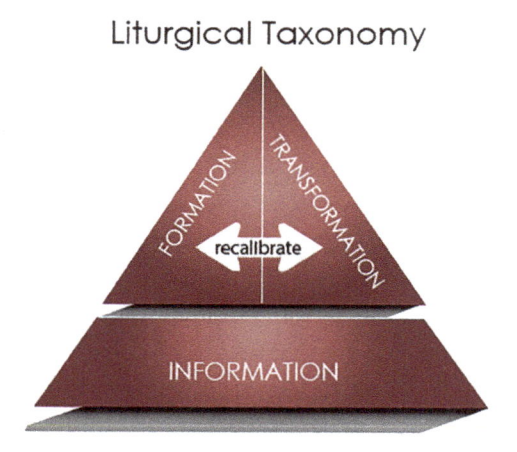

The question I like to ask those working with youth is, how much time are you spending guiding students through recalibration? As you step back and look at your ministry, how would your time break down between how much information you are sharing versus the formative experiences you are creating? As a parent, how much time are you actually spending intentionally recalibrating your child's heart? In my work with teachers and parents, it appears that our intentional formation time is significantly less than it should be.

Liturgical Taxonomy

RAISING CONTRIBUTORS
IN A CULTURE OF CONSUMERISM AND SKEPTICISM

Moving from remembering strategies on Bloom's to creating strategies is an important step, but moving from information to recalibration within the liturgical taxonomy is crucial when working with this generation of kids. As I move into practicalities and making meaning of all of this, it is important that we create more spaces and experiences for kids to live out these theoretical concepts. James K.A. Smith reminds us in John chapter 1 that Jesus asked two would-be disciples a very pointed question that He asks all of us, "What do you want?"

Jesus asks another form of this question to Peter in John 21 when He asks, "Do you love me?" He doesn't ask us what we know; He doesn't ask us what do we believe. He asks us what do we want? Do you love me? This is so devastating because our wants, longings, and desires are at the core of our being.

So maybe the most important question we could be asking is, are we forming the loves of our children to align with the love of Christ? To take a statement from earlier in the book, are we cultivating first things or second things? A teenage contributor, *Jaquelle Crowe*, wrote *The Gospel Changes Everything*, and she has these powerful words to tell each of us.

"Here's the inevitable truth: our hearts will always find something to worship, and that will motivate how we live. We live for what we glory in, what we worship." What love are we cultivating in our children? Our contributions are an overflow or outpouring of our loves.

In 2007, a twenty-year-old college student named Jonathon Reed submitted a poem to an AARP video contest. The submission requirements were to create a two-minute video describing their vision for the future. In a Reddit poll done in 2013, this poem won *most upvotes* of any poem. His submission was called "The Lost Generation."

The Lost Generation

I am part of a lost generation,
and I refuse to believe that
I can change the world

I realize this may be a shock but
'Happiness comes from within'
is a lie, and
'Money will make me happy'
So in thirty years I will tell my children
They are not the most important thing in my life.
My employer will know that
I have my priorities straight because
work is more important than
family
I tell you this
Once upon a time
Families stayed together
but this will not be true in my era
this is a quick fix society
Experts tell me
Thirty years from now I will be celebrating the
10th anniversary of my divorce
I do not concede that
I will live in a country of my own making
In the future
Environmental destruction will be the norm
No longer can it be said that
My peers and I care about this earth
It will be evident that
My generation is apathetic and lethargic
It is foolish to presume that
There is hope.

And all of this will come true unless we choose to reverse it.

Is it foolish to presume there is hope for this generation? I sure hope not, but some days, it seems pretty gloomy. I must admit, as I look around at the spiritual formation strategies we are using with kids, I often find myself frustrated. Frustrated because they are the same today as they were in the 1990s. In the early 2000s, a pioneer in faith research for children, George Barna, wrote a book called

RAISING CONTRIBUTORS
IN A CULTURE OF CONSUMERISM AND SKEPTICISM

Transforming Children into Spiritual Champions. In this book, he shared research from the late '90s that seemed to predict the future faith dilemma that we are seeing today.

Fairly soon after George Barna published his research, we saw another book come out titled *Almost Christian* by Kendra Dean. Kendra highlighted one of the largest faith studies ever done on youth and their feelings toward faith. Dr. Christian Smith led this research, and his findings were overwhelmingly in favor of seeing a future faith crisis with our kids. For over twenty years we have now been sitting on this data, we have seen the pitfalls, and yet we continue down the same path of spiritually forming our kids.

It doesn't have to be this way. As adults, we have the ability to rethink how we help our younger generations navigate the difficult and confusing world that lies ahead of them. Instead of expecting and fostering consumption, we can rise up and cultivate them as contributors to their world. Contributing their image-bearing nature to their neighbors. Contributing their Christlike spirit of hope and love. I certainly believe this is a generation for great opportunity and a group of difference makers ready to be unleashed of the low expectations we have for them.

Jonathan Reed didn't leave his poem without hope for the future. There is hope, he believes. Just read the poem backward now.

The Lost Generation

> There is hope.
> It is foolish to presume that
> My generation is apathetic and lethargic.
> It will be evident that
> My peers and I care about this Earth.
> No longer can it be said that
> Environmental destruction will be the norm.
> In the future,
> I will live in a country of my own making.
> I do not concede that

> Thirty years from now, I will be celebrating the
> tenth anniversary of my divorce.
> Experts tell me
> This is a quick fix society
> But this will not be true in my era.
> Families stayed together
> Once upon a time
> I'll tell you this:
> Family
> Is more important than
> Work
> I have my priorities straight because
> My employer will know that
> They are not the most important thing in my life.
> So in thirty years, I will tell my children
> "Money will make me happy"
> Is a lie, and
> "True Happiness comes from within"
> I realize this may be a shock, but
> I can change the world.
> And I refuse to believe that
> I am part of a lost generation.

They will and can change the world, but we must allow them to try. As churches and families, we must begin creating cultures that look more like incubators than prisons of low expectations. Incubators are safe places to learn, grow, and most importantly, fail. Incubators are places that launch greatness into the world; they are places that attempt to equip people with the necessary tools needed to make a difference, and they are places of empowerment, not protection. Let's be bold and take the safety devices off of our kids and allow them to begin navigating the world ahead of them in authentic and Christlike ways.

Let us be reminded by the words of Ellen Page from 1922:

> Oh, parents, parents everywhere, point out
> to us the ideals of truly glorious and upright liv-

ing! Believe in us, that we may learn to believe in ourselves, in humanity, in God! Be the living examples of your teachings, that you may inspire us with hope and courage, understanding and truth, love and faith. Remember that we are the parents of the future. Help us to be worthy of the sacred trust that will be ours. Make your lives such an inspiration to us that we in turn will strive to become an inspiration to our children and to the ages! Is it too much to ask?

Adults, it is our job to lead the next generation to love God and to follow Him. Let's humble ourselves and rise up to the calling He has given us to form faith in the lives of our kids. Our kids mirror our actions, and if we are not living into the Spirit, they will see that. The faith formation of our kids starts with our walk with God. Lean on God in prayer, trust in Him, and we can do this!

CHAPTER 10

The Playbook
How to Raise a Contributor

> When I was very young, most of my childhood heroes wore capes, flew through the air, or picked up buildings with one arm. They were spectacular and got a lot of attention. But as I grew, my heroes changed, so that now I can honestly say that anyone who does anything to help a child is a hero to me.
>
> —Mr. Rogers

This is a guide for raising children that contribute to their world. How do we move our children away from consumption and toward contribution? This guidebook walks you through five sections of creating a contributor plan for your family. These five sessions will cover

1. why does contribution matter;
2. identifying and fostering my child's gifts and loves;
3. prioritizing first things;
4. career and calling; and
5. goal setting.

What is expected of parents? There are so many cultural expectations for parents and pressures from so many sides. As a parent myself, I know the pressures of youth sports, academic excellence,

RAISING CONTRIBUTORS
IN A CULTURE OF CONSUMERISM AND SKEPTICISM

and all the pressures that go with your children's behaviors. I haven't found many expectations from the church for my parenting. Have you found this? What have been your experiences?

In the book, we focus on the origins of Scripture and humanity as we go back to a Genesis 1 mindset and way of thinking. It appears from the origins of Scripture God places faith formation in the hands of parents:

> Hear, O Israel: The Lord our God, the Lord is one. Love the Lord your God with all your heart and with all your soul and with all your strength. These commandments that I give you today are to be upon your *hearts. Impress them on your children. Talk about them when you sit at home and when you walk along the road, when you lie down and when you get up. Tie them as symbols on your hands and bind them on your foreheads. Write them on the doorframes of your houses and on your gates.* (Deuteronomy 6:4–7)

Why does God think parents should have this main responsibility and not the church or the school?

Dr. Glen Shultz, in his book *Kingdom Education*, argues that Satan understands that if he can attack the *home*, he will create a cultural obstacle in the faith formation of our children.

Satan's intent:

God's intent:

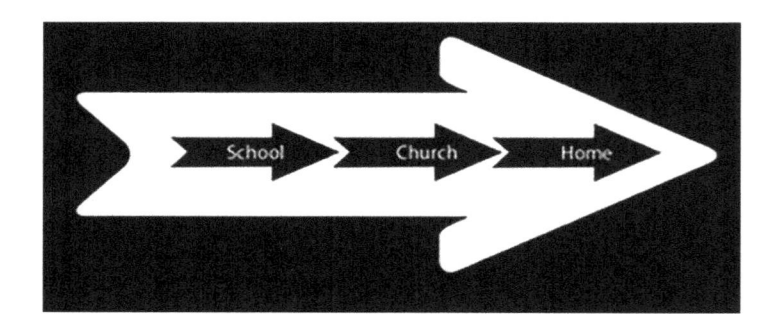

In this playbook, we will focus on all of the different parts of life that are shaping our children. Are we doing enough as parents to shape and ground our children? It is pretty evident that culture has low expectations for our children, and statistically, our children are living up to them. Our children are living in an age of *low expectations, mediocrity, little accountability,* and a *surface-level faith engagement.*

What expectations do you have for your children?

Session 1: Why does contribution matter?

https://www.arcgis.com/apps/MapJournal/index.html?appid=ac55ae1de8e94fba8a0147dee9ebe3fb

RAISING CONTRIBUTORS
IN A CULTURE OF CONSUMERISM AND SKEPTICISM

Erikson's Psychosocial Stages Summary Chart

Stage	Basic Conflict	Important Events	Key Questions to be answered	Outcome
Infancy (0 to 18 months)	Trust vs. Mistrust	Feeding/ Comfort	Is my world safe?	Children develop a sense of trust when caregivers provide reliability, care and affection. A lack of this will lead to mistrust.
Early Childhood (2 to 3)	Autonomy vs. Shame and Doubt	Toilet Training/ Dressing	Can I do things by myself or need I always rely on others?	Children need to develop a sense of personal control over physical skills and a sense of independence. Success leads to feeling of autonomy, failure results in feelings of shame and doubt.
Preschool (3 to 5)	Initiative vs. Guilt	Exploration/ Play	Am I good or bad?	Children need to begin asserting control and power over the environment. Success in this state leads to a sense of purpose. Children who try to exert too much power experience disapproval, resulting in a sense of guilt.
School Age (6 to 11)	Industry vs. Inferiority	School/ Activities	How can I be good?	Children need to cope with new social and academic demands. Success leads to a sense of competence, while failure results in feeling of inferiority.
Adolescence (12 to 18)	Identity vs. Role Confusion	Social Relationships/ Identity	Who am I and where am I going?	Teens need to develop a sense of self and personal identity. Success leads to an ability to stay true to yourself, while failure leads to role confusion and a weak sense of self.
Young Adult (19 to 40)	Intimacy vs. Isolation	Intimate Relationships	Am I loved and wanted?	Young adults need to form intimate, loving relationships with other people. Success leads to strong relationships, while failure results in loneliness and isolation.
Middle Adulthood (40 to 65)	Generativity vs. Stagnation	Work and Parenthood	Will I provide something of real value?	Adults need to create or nurture things that will outlast them, often by having children or creating a positive change that benefits other people. Success leads to feelings of usefulness and accomplishment, while failure results in shallow involvement in the world.
Maturity (65 to death)	Ego Identity vs. Despair	Reflection on life	Have I lived a full life?	Older adults need to look back on life and feel a sense of fulfillment. Success at this state leads to a feeling of wisdom, while failure results in regret, bitterness, and despair.

More than likely, you will have children between stages two to four. What commonalities do these stages have?

Erik Erikson highlights purpose and meaning as essential to development. Well, check this out!

> So God created mankind in his own image, in the image of God he created them; male and female he created them.
> The Lord God took the man and put him in the Garden of Eden to work it and take care of it. (Genesis 1:26; 2:15)

God created man, put him in the garden to _____ ____ and _____ _____ of it.

"working and taking care" = contribute

Two action words that God gave all of humanity. As a parent, what are you doing to foster contribution in your child? We are made to contribute and not to consume. In fact, the sin in the garden was fundamentally consumption. The desire to want something, to be like God.

Let's move our children from consumption to contribution. From wanting *meaningless stuff* to doing *meaningful stuff*.

Ask your child to make two lists:

1. What do you want? list
2. What do you want to do? list

Then determine how much of those lists are consumer minded versus consumption minded. When they think of doing, is it the mindset of entertainment or meaningful contribution? What would your lists look like?

Session 2: *What gifts do my children have?*

Use this drawing of a child and design it in a way that reflects your child. Draw in hair, shoes, clothes, and accessories.

NAME:_____

What do they love to do?

What are their struggles?

What are they best at doing?

RAISING CONTRIBUTORS
IN A CULTURE OF CONSUMERISM AND SKEPTICISM

Here is a chart from ysa.org that might help you think of different things your children are passionate about. Take a look at this chart and circle the areas in which you think your child shows interest. If they are really interested, put a double circle around it.

Music Playing an instrument, singing, writing songs.	Art Painting, drawing, sculpture, graphic art.	Writing Writing poetry, stories, and plays; journalism.	Movement Dancing, martial arts, cheerleading.
Building Wood working, construction, welding.	**Leadership** Peace building, student government, politics.	**Entrepreneurship** Business, marketing, inventing things.	**Sports** Team sports, physical activities, competitions.
Teaching Mentoring, tutoring, teaching, reading to kids.	Nature Exploring nature, wildlife, gardening.	Animals Caring for animals, training, medicine.	Computers Software development, repair, web design.
Creative Arts Cooking, sewing, fashion, knitting.	**Academic Subjects** Science, math, history, literature, geography.	**Speech** Debate or public speaking, broadcasting.	**Comedy** Making people laugh, jokes, writing sketches.
Spirituality Prayer, meditation, studying sacred texts.	Drama / Theater Acting, directing, theater lighting, or set design.	Photography & Film Taking pictures, making films, animation.	Reading Reading fiction, nonfiction, poetry.
Advocacy Politics and government, commitment to a cause	**Journalism** Newscasting, writing, radio & TV production.	**Outdoor Recreation** Fishing, hunting, hiking, camping, bicycling.	**Mechanics** Electronics or machine repair, auto repair.

Now let's start to take your child's desires and connect them to ways they can use those to honor God. How can you help your child bear God's image in the world? How can your child play a role in the redemption of the world?

THE GLOBAL GOALS
For Sustainable Development

1 NO POVERTY
2 ZERO HUNGER
3 GOOD HEALTH AND WELL-BEING
4 QUALITY EDUCATION
5 GENDER EQUALITY
6 CLEAN WATER AND SANITATION
7 AFFORDABLE AND CLEAN ENERGY
8 DECENT WORK AND ECONOMIC GROWTH
9 INDUSTRY, INNOVATION AND INFRASTRUCTURE
10 REDUCED INEQUALITIES
11 SUSTAINABLE CITIES AND COMMUNITIES
12 RESPONSIBLE CONSUMPTION AND PRODUCTION
13 CLIMATE ACTION
14 LIFE BELOW WATER
15 LIFE ON LAND
16 PEACE, JUSTICE AND STRONG INSTITUTIONS
17 PARTNERSHIPS FOR THE GOALS

THE GLOBAL GOALS
For Sustainable Development

You can find more information about each of these areas on the 17 Global Goals website. What are the goals that your child would have empathy for or would have interest in?

What nonprofits or groups are in your area that focus on your answers? Call them and ask how you and your child can engage in these issues. God calls your child to bear God's image today, not once they graduate. Get your child engaged in the redemption of the world early.

Where do you think your child sees pain in the world?

Here is another chart from www.ysa.org to help you look at problems from a different perspective. How do some of these problems connect with the 17 Global Goals? Would your child care about helping with any of these areas?

Education	Bullying/Violence	Dropout Prevention	Disasters
Recruit and train ____ volunteer readers, tutors, and mentors.	Reduce bullying and/or violence in school and communities by ____%.	Encourage ____ students to stay in school.	Help ____ people to prepare for a disaster.
Safe Driving	**Water**	**Reduce, Reuse, Recycle**	**Energy**
Educate ____ people about the dangers of distracted driving.	Restore or protect ____ bodies of water.	Keep ____ pounds of glass, metal, plastic, or paper out of landfills.	Help save energy and reduce your carbon footprint by ____%.
Hunger	**Economic Opportunity**	**First Aid**	**Gender Equality**
Provide food for ____ people.	Organize a job skills training for ____ people.	Work with local agencies to train ____ people in CPR/first aid skills.	Speak out for gender rights to empower ____ people.
Access to School	**Trees**	**Places to Play**	**Green Space**
Help ____ students around the world attend school or gain access to the internet.	Increase the Earth's tree cover by planting ____ trees.	Create or improve ____ playgrounds to provide safe places for children to play.	Create ____ square feet of new green spaces or community gardens.
Biodiversity	**Health & Obesity**	**Disease**	**Housing**
Protect ____ acres of habitat for endangered plant and animal species.	Increase physical activity and / or healthy eating habits of ____ people.	Stop the spread of infectious diseases by immunizing or educating ____ people..	Build or renovate ____ affordable housing units.
Healthier Babies	**Destructive Decisions**	**Medical Research**	**Other Cause**
Prevent premature birth, and improve the health of ____ moms and babies.	Reduce the use of drugs, alcohol, tobacco, or risky sexual behavior by ____%.	Raise ____ dollars to support research to cure or treat diseases.	Add another issue you care about:

Session 3: *Practicing first things*

> You can only get first things first by putting second things second.
>
> (C.S. Lewis)

RAISING CONTRIBUTORS
IN A CULTURE OF CONSUMERISM AND SKEPTICISM

Let's examine how your child spends their time in a given week. What fills up their days? Look at the key below the chart and fill in the schedule accordingly.

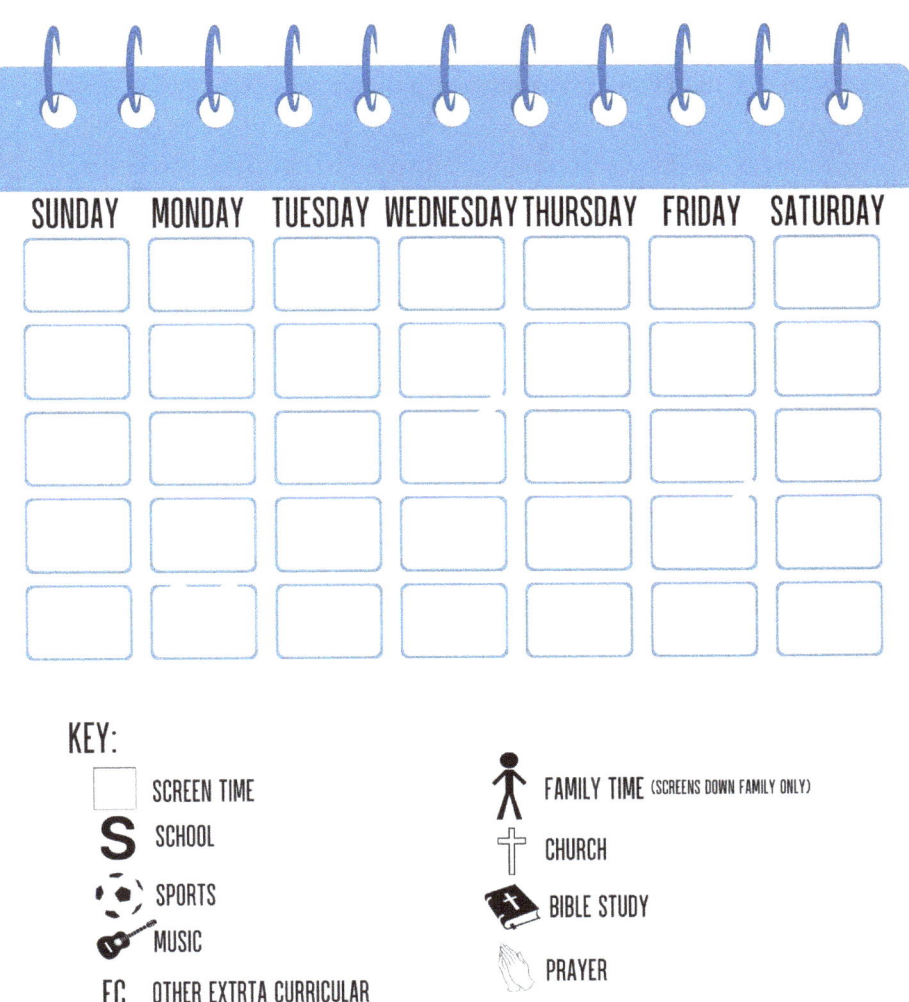

SUNDAY	MONDAY	TUESDAY	WEDNESDAY	THURSDAY	FRIDAY	SATURDAY

KEY:
- ☐ SCREEN TIME
- S SCHOOL
- ⚽ SPORTS
- 🎸 MUSIC
- EC OTHER EXTRTA CURRICULAR
- 🚶 FAMILY TIME (SCREENS DOWN FAMILY ONLY)
- ✝ CHURCH
- 📖 BIBLE STUDY
- 🙏 PRAYER

Use the key and fill in the calendar with an average week of how you spend your time with your children.

Next, let's look at how you as a parent or guardian spend time praising your child.

CELEBRATION CHART

Fill in this pie chart. Look at the categories below and decide how much time you spend praising or celebrating your child for those particualr behaviors. If there are categories missing feel free to add to the chart.

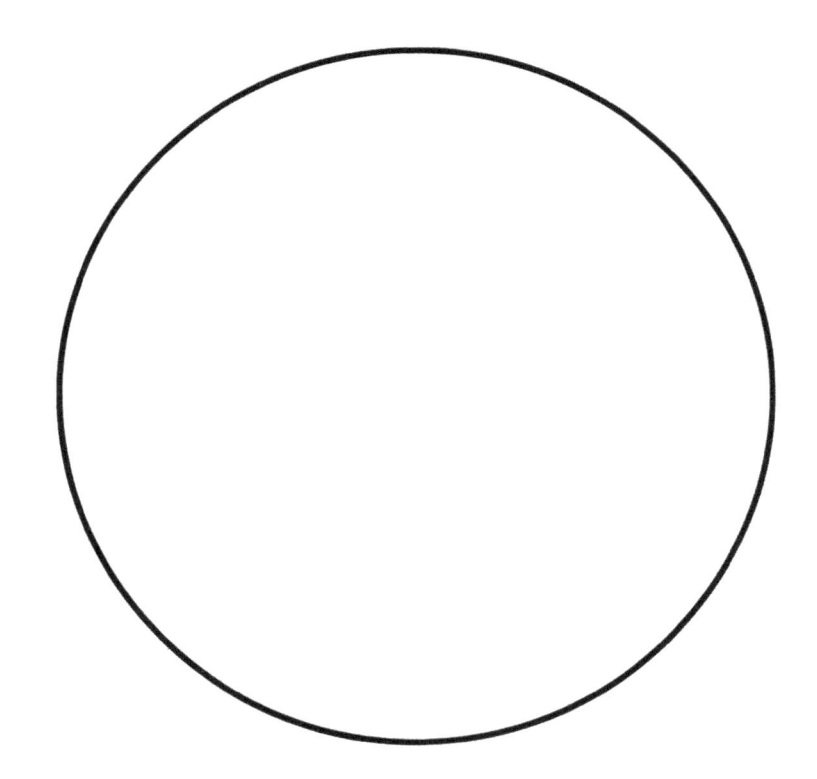

- Athletics
- Music
- Theater
- Spiritual Disciplines
- Work Ethic
- Integrity
- Academics
- Kindness

RAISING CONTRIBUTORS
IN A CULTURE OF CONSUMERISM AND SKEPTICISM

What are the top three areas in which your child spends their time?

1.
2.
3.

What are your top two areas you praise your child most?

1.
2.

How do these align with first things, and how can you do better on focusing on first things?

Similarly, to the picture you drew in session 2, now draw a picture of what you want to see when your child is thirty years old.

NAME:_____

What will they dress like?

What will their job be?

What character traits will they have ?

What are you doing in your calendar or your celebration chart for your child to live up to your thirty-year-old image? A friend of mine told me his twenty-year-old daughter asked him why he never talked to her about being a mom. He always talked to her about careers. It is important to remember that the most important thing many of our children will end up doing is raise a child. Sometimes the most important thing we do for the kingdom is not something we do but someone we raise. Let's not forget we are raising moms and dads.

PROTECTION VS EMPOWERMENT
indicate where you are at on each of the likert scale questions:

in your parenting where do you seee yourself on this spectrum?

overprotected — empowered

Please complete the questions relevant to the ages of your children.

3 YEARS OLD - 12 YEARS OLD

i let my kids play outside without watching them.

1 2 3 4 5
Never — Always

i encourage my kids to do things they are not good at.

1 2 3 4 5
Never — Always

I celebrate failure with my children.

1 2 3 4 5
Never — Always

I get my children ready for school.

1 2 3 4 5
Never — Always

RAISING CONTRIBUTORS
IN A CULTURE OF CONSUMERISM AND SKEPTICISM

Please complete the questions relevant to the ages of your children.

13 YEARS OLD - 18 YEARS OLD

i have a curfew for my child.

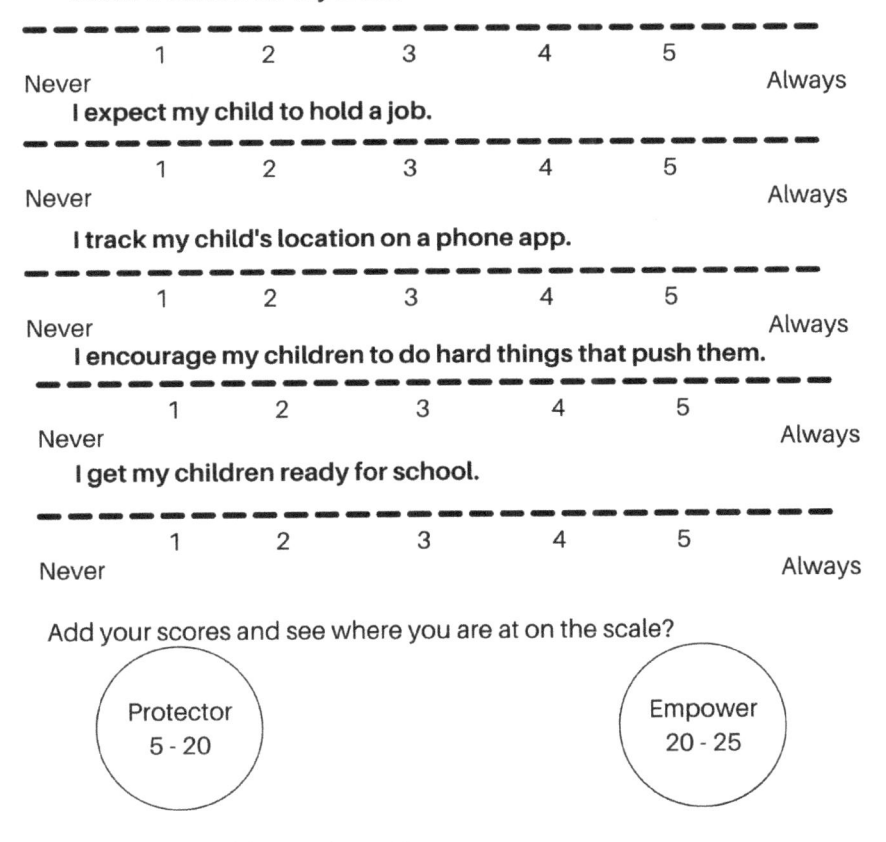

```
         1        2        3        4        5
Never                                                   Always
```

I expect my child to hold a job.

```
         1        2        3        4        5
Never                                                   Always
```

I track my child's location on a phone app.

```
         1        2        3        4        5
Never                                                   Always
```

I encourage my children to do hard things that push them.

```
         1        2        3        4        5
Never                                                   Always
```

I get my children ready for school.

```
         1        2        3        4        5
Never                                                   Always
```

Add your scores and see where you are at on the scale?

(Protector 5 - 20)   (Empower 20 - 25)

Do you agree? Why or why not?

Session 4: Career and purpose

This section is just as important whether your child is in first grade or twelfth grade. In fact, the younger the better. Often, when young parents see career topics for their kids, they tend to dismiss it. However, as we see with the eight life stages, work and purpose are critical to our children's development. Remember we are raising functional adults, not just happy kids.

Go back to section 2. What gifts does your child have? What careers would be a good fit? Also, what careers has your child mentioned wanting to do? List them out:

1.
2.
3.
4.
5.

Now take this list and write down a Christian you know in each of those professions.

1.
2.
3.
4.
5.

How can you set up a moment for your child to visit with these people individually? Can you take your child out of school one day to meet them at their office and let your child learn about their work? Here are some great questions:

1. What do you do?
2. How did you prepare for this job?
3. What is hard about your job?
4. What is something that surprised you about your job?
5. What is fun about your job?
6. How do you show Christ in your job?

RAISING CONTRIBUTORS
IN A CULTURE OF CONSUMERISM AND SKEPTICISM

What camps or programs exist to foster your children's gifts? Often we think of sports camps, but stretch yourself here. Here are some examples:

1. Zoo camps
2. Computer coding camp
3. Robotics camps
4. Biblical leadership camps
5. Public speaking/debate

How can you get your child involved in these?

Based on the age of your child, have them do the following exercises:

- Three years old to eight years old
    Draw a picture of what you want to be when you grow up.
- Nine years old to twelve years old
    Write a story about what you will do when you grow up.
- Thirteen years old to eighteen years old
    Write a paper or create a video telling Mom and Dad what you will do when you grow up. Why are you going to do this? What will you need to do to make sure you're able to do this? How will you honor God in this work?

Once this happens, save it. On birthdays, use this and talk about it. If they move into a new age bracket, have them update it using that activity. Here are good follow-up questions with your kids:

1. How will you be like Jesus in your job?
2. How will you be a contributor for Jesus in your job?
3. What excites you about your job?
4.

Session 5: Goal setting

Create a goal-setting document for your kids. Once they fill it out, you should put it in their rooms. Here are the components:

Name: _____
Grade:_____
My word for the year: _____
These are the new things I want to try this year:
1.
2.
3.

These are the things I want to finish this year:
1.
2.
3.

One fear I will work to overcome this year:
1.

Three things I will do this year that will push me out of my comfort zone:
1.
2.
3.

Three things I need from my parents this year:
1.
2.
3.

BIBLIOGRAPHY

Bell, Rob. *Velvet Elvis: Repainting the Christian Faith*. HarperOne, 2012.
Crouch, Andy. *Culture Making: Recovering Our Creative Calling*. IVP Books, 2013.
Crowe, Jaquelle. *This Changes Everything: How the Gospel Transforms the Teen Years*. Crossway, 2017.
Dean, Kenda Creasy. *Almost Christian: What the Faith of Our Teenagers Is Telling the American Church*. Oxford University Press, 2010.
Duckworth, Angela. *Grit: The Power of Passion and Perseverance*. Scribner, 2016.
Elmore, Tim. *Artificial Maturity: Helping Kids Meet the Challenge of Becoming Authentic Adults*. Jossey-Bass, 2012.
Enns, Peter. *The Bible Tells Me So: Why Defending Scripture Has Made Us Unable to Read It*. HarperOne, 2014.
Harris, Alex, and Brett Harris. *Do Hard Things: A Teenage Rebellion against Low Expectations*. Multnomah Books, 2017.
Kantorová, K., Jonášová, H., Panuš, J., & Lipka, R. "A Study of Generation Z from the Communication Perspective of Universities." *Scientific papers of the University of Pardubice, Series D, Faculty of Economics and Administration* 40 (2017): 83–94. Retrieved from http://hdl.handle.net/10195/67927
Keller, Timothy, and Katherine L. Alsdorf. *Every Good Endeavor: Connecting Your Work to God's Work*. 2016.
Kinnaman, David. *Gen Z: The Culture, Beliefs and Motivations Shaping the Next Generation*. 2018.

Lewis, Robert. *Raising a Modern-Day Knight: A Father's Role in Guiding His Son to Authentic Manhood*. Focus on the Family, 2007.

Lythcott-Haims, Julie. *How to Raise an Adult: Break Free of the Overparenting Trap and Prepare Your Kid for Success*. Henry Hold and Co., 2015.

Magonet, Jonathan. *A Rabbi Reads the Torah*. SCM Press, 2013.

Magonet, Jonathan. *A Rabbi Reads the Bible*. Hymns Ancient & Modern Ltd., 2004.

Ong, Walter J. *Orality and Literacy, The Technologizing of the World*. New York, NY: Routledge, Taylor and Francis Group, 2005.

Raynor, Jordan. *Called to Create: A Biblical Invitation to Create, Innovate, and Risk*. Baker Books, 2017.

Root, Andrew. *The Pastor in a Secular Age: Ministry to People Who No Longer Need a God*. Baker Academic, 2019.

Sasse, Ben. *The Vanishing American Adult: Our Coming-of-Age Crisis—and How to Rebuild a Culture of Self-Reliance*. St. Martin's Press, 2017.

Sax, Leonard. *The Collapse of Parenting: How We Hurt Our Kids When We Treat Them Like Grown-Ups*.

Smith, James. *You Are What You Love: The Spiritual Power of Habit*. Brazos Press, 2016.

Taylor, Charles. *A Secular Age*. Belknap Press, 2018.

Taylor, Larry. *Running with the Horses: A Parenting Guide for Raising Children to be Servant-Leaders for Christ*. WestBow Press, 2013.

Tough, Paul. *How Children Succeed: Grit, Curiosity, and the Hidden Power of Character*. Mariner Books, 2012.

Turner, J. C., Brown, R. J., & Tajfel, H. "Social Comparison and Group Interest in Ingroup Favouritism." *European Journal of Social Psychology* 9, no. 2 (1979): 187–204. doi:10.1002/ejsp.2420090207.

Wendham, Gordon. *Story as Torah: Reading Old Testament Narrative Ethically*. Baker Academic, 2012.

Niels Ebdrup. "The Origin of Fiction." ScienceNordic. September 12, 2012. https://sciencenordic.com/christianity-denmark-history/the-origin-of-fiction/1376193.

https://iid.co/.

http://talesofakansasfarmmom.blogspot.com/2013/02/just-farm-kid-guest-post.html

https://www.ncps-k12.org/cms/lib/CT01903077/Centricity/Domain/638/Poem%20- %20Lost%20Generation%20-%20Text.pdf.

https://www.arcgis.com/apps/MapJournal/index.html?appid=ac55ae1de8e94fba8a0147dee9e 4684 be3fb

https://www.amazon.com/Artificial-Maturity-Challenge-Becoming-Authentic/dp/1118258061.

https://www.christianbook.com/sticky-faith-kara-powell/9780310329329/pd/329320?dv=%7Bdevice%7D&en=google&event=SHOP&kw=church-and-pastoral-0-20%7C329320&p=1179710&gclid=Cj0KCQjwkZfLBRCzARIsAH3wMKpgktN-1c_GpAnTcmXKWH58YUSIgd4edLJMa8H0iGd2UO0ERRc6-CMaAiUsEALw_wcB.

https://growingleaders.com/blog/ambition-comes-incentive/.

http://websupport1.citytech.cuny.edu/Faculty/pcatapano/US2/US%20Documents/flappersappeal.html.

http://parentingteens.about.com/od/behavioranddiscipline/ht/delegate_teen.htm

John Piper, "Why Did God Create the World?" Desiring God, September 22, 2012, https://www.desiringgod.org/messages/why-did-god-create-the-world.

Keller, Timothy, and Katherine L. Alsdorf. *Every Good Endeavor: Connecting Your Work to God's Work.* 2016.

Ong, Walter J. *Orality and Literacy, The Technologizing of the World.* New York, NY: Routledge, Taylor and Francis Group, 2005.

https://hopestillfloats.files.wordpress.com/2016/02/adam-in-the-garden-of-eden.jpg

https://reproarte.com/en/choice-of-topics/style/baroque/first-work-of-adam-and-eve-detail

ABOUT THE AUTHOR

Dr. Brandon Tatum serves in the Executive Branch of the state of Oklahoma government as the chief of staff for Governor Kevin Stitt. Prior to his role in the government, Dr. Tatum spent fifteen years working in Christian higher education and Christian K-12. Previously, he served as the executive vice president and chief strategy officer for Oklahoma Christian University. Dr. Tatum has been recognized for his work in educational innovation and strategy. He served on the Oklahoma governor's education committee, focusing on personalized learning and innovation, and served as the governor's appointee on the Oklahoma Statewide Virtual Learning Commission.

He serves on or has served on the following boards: Council of American Private Education Commission, the Texas Private School Accreditation Commission, Oklahoma Private School Accreditation Commission, and the National Christian School Association. Previously, he served as the superintendent for Oklahoma Christian Academy and the executive director of the National Christian School Association. He is the author of two children's books, *The Adventures of Grit* and the *Diary of a Lousy Book*. Brandon and his wife Megan have an eight-year-old son named Sawyer and five-year-old twin daughters Blakely and Gentry.

CPSIA information can be obtained
at www.ICGtesting.com
Printed in the USA
BVHW061558070423
661951BV00022B/837